R. P. Stout

Official Correspondence Relating to the Admission of Montana as a State Into the Union

and other official papers comprising correspondence with the State and War Departments, at Washington, and including proclamations and official addresses of Jos.

R. P. Stout

Official Correspondence Relating to the Admission of Montana as a State Into the Union

and other official papers comprising correspondence with the State and War Departments, at Washington, and including proclamations and official addresses of Jos.

ISBN/EAN: 9783337734015

Printed in Europe, USA, Canada, Australia, Japan

Cover: Foto ©Andreas Hilbeck / pixelio.de

More available books at **www.hansebooks.com**

Official Correspondence

RELATING TO THE

Admission of Montana as a State into the Union

AND OTHER OFFICIAL PAPERS COMPRISING
CORRESPONDENCE WITH THE

State and War Departments,

AT WASHINGTON,

AND INCLUDING

Proclamations and Official Addresses

OF

JOS. K. TOOLE,

(GOVERNOR OF THE STATE OF MONTANA.)

COMPILED BY

R. P. STOUT,

PRIVATE SECRETARY TO THE GOVERNOR.

DEC. 31, 1892.

HELENA, MONTANA :
C. K. WELLS COMPANY, PRINTERS AND BINDERS,
1892.

The Day and Hour when Montana was Admitted into the Union.

EXECUTIVE MANSION, WASHINGTON, D. C., Nov. 8, 1889.

To Hon. Jos. K. Toole,

Governor of the State of Montana, Helena, Mont.:

The President signed and issued the proclamation declaring Montana a State in the Union at 10 o'clock and 40 minutes, this morning.

JAMES G. BLAINE,
Secretary of State.

Official Papers, Executive Office.

Proclamation of Admission.

DEPT. OF STATE, WASHINGTON, D. C., Nov. 11, 1889.

To His Excellency, the Governor of Montana, Helena, Mont.:

SIR:—I have the honor to transmit herewith a duly authenticated copy of the President's Proclamation of November 8, 1889, admitting the State of Montana into the Union. I have the honor to be, sir, Your obedient servant,

JAMES G. BLAINE,
Secretary of State.

A PROCLAMATION BY THE PRESIDENT OF THE UNITED STATES OF AMERICA.

WHEREAS, The Congress of the United States did, by an act approved on the 22d day of February, 1889, provide that the inhabitants of the Territory of Montana might, upon the conditions prescribed in said act, become the State of Montana; and,

WHEREAS, It was provided by said act that delegates elected as therein provided, to a Constitutional Convention in the Territory of Montana, should meet at the seat of government of said Territory and that, after they had met and organized they should declare on behalf of the people of Montana that they adopt the Constitution of the United States; whereupon the said convention should be authorized to form a State government for the proposed State of Montana; and

WHEREAS, It was provided by said act that the Constitution so adopted should be republican in form and make no distinction in civil or political rights on account of race or color, except as to Indians not taxed, and not be repugnant to the Constitution of the United States and the principles of the Declaration of Independence; and that the Convention should by an ordinance irrevocable without the consent of the United States, and the people of said State, make certain provisions prescribed in said act; and,

WHEREAS, It was provided by said act that the Constitution thus formed for the people of Montana should, by an ordinance of the Constitution forming the same, be submitted to the people of Montana at an election, to be held therein on the first Tuesday in October, 1889, for ratification or rejection by the qualified voters of said proposed State ; and that the returns of said election should be made to the Secretary of the said Territory who, with the Governor and Chief Justice thereof, or any two of them, should canvass the same; and if a majority of the legal votes cast should be for the Constitution, the Governor should certify the result to the President of the United States, together with a statement of the votes cast thereon, and upon separate articles or propositions, and a copy of said Constitution, articles, propositions and ordinances ; and,

WHEREAS, It has been certified to me by the Governor of said Territory that, within the time prescribed by said act of Congress, a Constitution for the proposed State of Montana has been adopted, and that the same, together with two ordinances connected therewith, has been ratified by a majority of the qualified voters of said proposed State in accordance with the conditions prescribed in said act ; and,

WHEREAS, A duly authenticated copy of said Constitution and ordinances, as required by said act, has been received by me.

Now, therefore, I, Benjamin Harrison, President of the United States of America, do, in accordance with the provisions of the act of Congress aforesaid, declare and proclaim the fact that the conditions imposed by Congress on the State of Montana to entitle that State to admission to the Union have been ratified and accepted, and that the admission of the said State into the Union is now complete.

In testimony whereof, I have hereunto set my hand and caused the seal of the United States to be affixed.

[SEAL.] Done at the city of Washington, this 8th day of November, in the year of our Lord, 1889, and of the Independence of the United States of America, the one hundred and fourteenth.

BENJAMIN HARRISON.

By the President:
    JAMES G. BLAINE,
      Secretary of State.

Proclamation Convening the First Legislative Assembly of the State of Montana.

STATE OF MONTANA, } ss.
EXECUTIVE OFFICE,

HELENA, MONTANA, Nov. 11th, 1889.

WHEREAS, On the 8th day of November, A. D. 1889, a Proclamation was signed and issued by the President of the United States declaring Montana a State in the Union.

NOW, THEREFORE, I, Jos. K. Toole, Governor of the State of Montana, by virtue of the power and authority in me vested by the Constitution, do hereby convene the first regular session of the Legislative Assembly of the State of Montana, to meet at Helena, the seat of government of said State, on Saturday, November 23d, A. D. 1889, at 12 o'clock noon.

[SEAL.]

IN TESTIMONY WHEREOF, I have hereunto set my hand and caused the seal of the State of Montana to be affixed at Helena, the seat of government of said State, this 11th day of November, A. D. 1889.

JOS. K. TOOLE.

By the Governor:
L. ROTWITT,
Secretary of State.

Proclamation.

STATE OF MONTANA, } ss.
EXECUTIVE OFFICE, }

HELENA, MONTANA, Nov. 22d, 1889.

WHEREAS, On the 11th day of November, A. D. 1889, a Proclamation was signed and issued convening the First Legislative Assembly of the State of Montana at the seat of government on Saturday, November 23d. 1889, at 12 o'clock noon ; and

WHEREAS, No provision of the Constitution or of the laws provide the place in which the said Legislative Asssmbly shall meet, and no officer or person is expressly authorized by the Constitution or the laws to designate such place of meeting ; and

WHEREAS, It is necessary that some suitable and convenient place of meeting shall be designated and provided ; and

WHEREAS, It has come to my knowledge that two sets of certificates have been issued to persons claiming to be elected to said Legislative Assembly, each emanating from a different source, and not all to the same persons ; and

WHEREAS, It is probable that a conflict may arise between the respective claimants to seats in said body, and in the organization thereof, which may imperil the peace of the State ; and

WHEREAS. One set of said certiffcates has been issued and delivered pursuant to Section 1033 of the General Election Laws of Montana, by the County Clerks of the respective Counties, and by virtue of Section 18 of an Act of the Legislative Assembly of the Territory of Montana, entitled " An Act to provide for the Registration of the Names ot Electors, and to Prevent Fraud at Elections," approved March 8th, A. D. 1889 ; and

WHEREAS, By express law, the persons holding such certificates are declared to be entitled to membership and deemed to be elected for all purposes of organization of either branch of the Legislative Assembly; and

WHEREAS, When so organized such Legislative Assembly, by the Constitution, becomes the judge of the qualifications of its own members;

NOW, THEREFORE, I, Jos. K. Toole, Governor of the State of Montana, do hereby designate the Court House of the County of Lewis and Clarke, at the said seat of government, as the place where said Legislative Assembly, comprising the persons holding and presenting certificates of election from said County Clerks shall meet, to-wit: The House of Representatives shall meet in the Hall formerly occupied by the Territorial House of Representatives, and the Senate shall meet in the Chamber formerly occupied by the Territorial Council.

For the observance of this Proclamation I invoke the aid of all good citizens, without distinction of party.

IN TESTIMONY WHEREOF, I have hereunto set my hand and caused the seal of the State of Montana to be affixed at Helena, the seat of government of said State, the 22d day of November, in the year of our Lord one thousand eight hundred and eighty-nine.

[SEAL.]

JOS. K. TOOLE.

By the Governor:
L. ROTWITT,
Secretary of State.

Governor's Message to First Legislative Assembly.

To the President of the Senate, and the Speaker of the House of Representatives:

Constitutional government has been conferred on us, and for the first time we undertake the management and control of our own affairs. The responsibility rests with us. It is in our power to make this the great State of the union, or to hamper and dwarf it for all time. In view of the difficulties which have attended the convening of the first legislative assembly under a Constitution, I yield the opportunity which precedent has established to indulge in patriotic sentiment which such an occasion, under different circumstances might inspire. I am content to congratulate you and the country upon the acquisition of another commonwealth of such magnificent proportions and great possibilities. The grandeur of wealth with which prodigal nature has endowed her, and the intelligence and aspirations of her people, preverifies my prediction that financially and politically Montana will be a column of strength in the national fabric, supporting with sturdy might her share of the public burdens, and forming an element of national greatness

Letter of Instruction to Captain John Smith.

STATE OF MONTANA, } ss.
EXECUTIVE OFFICE.

HELENA, Nov. 23, 1892.

SIR: At 12 o'clock, noon, to-day, you will open the doors to the House of Representatives and admit no person to the floor except persons claiming to be members of that body.

When notified by any member whom you have admitted that the House of Representatives is temporarily organized, you will turn over your keys to such person as the House may designate. If the Auditor of State appears at the door before you are released, by the person designated by the House of Representatives, you will admit him to the floor of the House.

When you are released by such person your employment ceases.

JOS. K. TOOLE,
Governor.

An Open Letter, Printed in the Daily Independent and Sent to the Governor's Office.

Helena Independent, December 1, 1889:

On Friday afternoon, November 22, it was apparent that there was a determination on the part of both republicans and democrats to take possession of the Court House and hold it for the purpose of organizing the House of Representatives. The United States Marshal was in the city and it was rumored that he had sworn in a large number of deputies and that several persons had proffered their services to lead an attack upon the Court House if the democrats sought to hold possession as against those republicans who did not have certificates from County Clerks. Some democrats were expressing a similar determination on their part. During the afternoon of that day several delegations waited upon Governor Toole, and brought the above facts to his attention, and gave it as their opinion that if the contending claimants should meet at the Court House in the absence of a proclamation from the Governor designating that place as the place for the meeting of the House of Representatives that both parties would assume the right to the exclusive occupancy of the building and a riot would ensue. It was urged that the power of the Executive was plenary to see that the persons holding and presenting the county certificates (being the lawful certificates), and no other persons, should be permitted to enter the legislative hall. Thereupon Governor Toole said that nothwithstanding what had been urged he would not exercise or attempt to exercise any such authority, but that in his opinion the county certificates were *prima facie* evidence of membership, and that persons holding such under the law were entitled to temporarily organize the House, and that under the circumstances he would declare that to be the law and designate the Court House as the place for the meeting of such, but that he would not under any circumstances undertake to prevent any person claiming to be a member of the House of Representatives from meeting at such place, no matter what sort of certificate he held. In this determination he was unalterable. He then said to us that he intended to issue a proclamation which he read to us. It was the same one issued and published on Saturday morning. We heard read in the House of Representatives the following letter. (Here follows Governor Toole's letter to Capt. Smith). This letter is in keeping with what Governor Toole said to us just before the proclamation was issued. We make this statement in justice to Governor Toole, whose action has been criticised by the very persons against whose presence in the House of Representatives he refused to interpose objections. The proclamation of the Governor was timely, and in our opinion was the means of preventing a breach of the peace, if not more serious consequences.

W. A. CLARK,
MARTIN MAGINNIS,
JOHN R. TOOLE,
W. M. THORNTON,
WALTER COOPER.

which can but redound to the honor and glory of the Republic. We were uniformly prosperous as a Territory, and starting out under such favorable auspices our progress ought to be phenomenal. Having full confidence in your ability to provide the necessary machinery to put the State Government in operation, and being fully assured of your patriotic desire in that respect, I promise you my active and cordial co-operation to that end.

In obedience to a constitutional provision, I now lay before you such information of the State as I possess, and certain recommendations for your consideration.

FINANCIAL CONDITION.

After the payment of all outstanding claims and indebtedness of every character, I think the State will, on January 1st, ensuing, have a small amount, not exceeding five thousand dollars, in the treasury. Our exact financial condition, together with an estimate of the amount necessary to defray all expenses for the ensuing two years, will be presented hereafter.

LEGISLATION REQUIRED BY THE CONSTITUTION.

I call your attention generally to the following sections of the Constitution which require legislative action to give them effect:

Sec. 15, article 3; section 23, article 3; sections 4, 5, 28, 30, 42 and 43, article 5; section 2, article 2; sections 2, 8, 9, 17 and 20, article 7; sections 4, 9, 19 and 32, article 8; sections 1 and 5, article 10; sections 1, 4, 6, 10 and 11, article 11; sections 1, 13 and 15, article 12; sections 5 and 6, article 13; sections 2, 3 and 4, article 14; sections 4, 7 and 20, article 15; sections 1 and 3, article 17; section 1, article 18; sections 3, 4 and 7, article 19.

The legislation suggested by many of these citations is of paramount importance, and without which the wheels of government will be clogged.

THE PENITENTIARY.

The penitentiary, formerly belonging to and under the control of the United States, has now become the property of the State. The same, with the lands connected therewith, were granted to the State by the act providing for our admission into the union. Under our territorial organization, the control and management of this institution was under the exclusive jurisdiction of the United States, with whom the Territory contracted for the maintenance and support of its prisoners. In providing for the change from Territorial to state government, no provision was made to cover the period between the date of admission and the time when the legislature should provide for the proper management of the same. Temporarily the United States Marshal is in charge, under the contract between the Territory and the United States. It is therefore important that you should make early provision for its government and maintenance. I therefore recommend that a Warden be provided, who may be authorized to employ such guards and assistants as you may deem proper, who shall have the control and management of the penitentiary under proper restrictions subject to the supervision of the Board of State Prison Commissioners. On the 10th day of October, A. D. 1889, the United States Marshal reported to Governor B. F. White, late Governor of Montana Territory, that there were confined in the penitentiary one hundred and seventy-three convicts, and that that number would be greatly increased rather than diminished in the future. The capacity of the penitentiary is only for one hundred and forty persons. It is therefore apparent that the present overcrowded condition of this institution is a constant menace to the security of the persons confined therein, as well as dangerous, from a sanitary point of view. The present United States Marshal, whose opportunities for observation have been superior to mine, and whose judgment is worthy of great consideration, in a communication to Governor White, under date of October 10th, 1889, says:

"In order to be of some use to you and to the legislature, I would most respectfully suggest as absolute necessities: The construction of a new cell house to contain at least forty-eight double cells, in size eight feet by ten; a suitable kitchen, with dining room for officers and one for prisoners; a warden's house; a system of steam heat; a system of sewerage, and other minor improvements. Around the whole, enclosing so much as deemed proper of the twenty acres of land granted by the United States, should be built a strong, suitable prison wall.

"I believe the whole of this can be done out of an appropriation of forty thousand dollars, and I know of no investment the Territory can make to its better advantage.

"Should matters remain in the condition they are, the force of guards will soon have to be largely increased to insure the custody of the prisoners. There is now paid out for guard hire about thirteen hundred dollars per month. The interest on forty thousand dollars would be about three hundred dollars per month. Every additional guard costs, at the government rate of pay for salary and board, about one hundred and five dollars per month; there ought to be added at least two more guards, and had the United States retained control of the penitentiary, my request therefor would have been granted. There are about twenty prisoners confined in an improvised jail building situated within the prison yard, and perilous as it is, they, and many others to come, must be confined this way until the legislature meets the exigency of the situation. Unless prompt and efficient aid is given to the State management of the penitentiary, a wholesale delivery is not among the grave improbabilities. The shot gun and rifle is just now the most necessary auxiliary in the detention of bad characters confined in the Montana penitentiary."

Without endorsing these recommendations, I commit the subject to your careful consideration and investigation, with the hope that speedy and proper legislation may be had on this subject.

INSANE.

The insane of the State are supported under a contract between the Territory of Montana and Doctors Mitchell and Mussigbrod, at Warm Springs, Deer Lodge county, at $8 per week, making an expense to the State of about seventy-five thousand dollars per annum. The number is increasing rapidly, the last report showing 184 patients maintained at public expense. The maintenance of the insane and the penitentiary will form the largest items of expense under our State government. The proper treatment of those unfortunates committed to the asylum at the least possible expense to the State, calls for the exercise of your best judgment. I am not prepared at this time to say that any new arrangements would be advantageous to the State, or to the persons confined therein, but in view of the great and growing expense in that behalf, I urge the most thorough investigation of the subject.

STATE MILITIA.

Section 3, Article 14, of the Constitution makes it incumbent upon the State to maintain the militia by appropriation from the State treasury. In view of this provision and the great drain which this organization is making upon the treasury, it becomes a question of the greatest concern how to maintain the militia so as to preserve its efficiency in case of danger, and at the same time reduce the expense to the minimum. I submit that all salaries per diem and other extraordinary expenses must be materially reduced if not entirely done away with. The annual encampments now provided for by law may be beneficial as a matter of discipline to officers and men, but I cannot believe that the advantage is at all commensurate with the expense to the people. It is obvious that with the new burdens of expense which a State government imposes and which are absolutely necessary to the administration of its affairs, the most rigid economy must be practiced in every department of government.

The expense of the State Militia or National Guard as far as can be ascertained for the past year, including the building of an arsenal, will amount to $48,000 an increase over last year of about $32,000.

I commend this subject to your careful consideration, and earnestly hope that you may find it practicable to materially reduce the expense of this organization without impairing its usefulness. This, it seems to me, may be effected in the manner above suggested, and by repealing the law providing for annual encampments.

STATE INSTITUTIONS AND PUBLIC BUILDINGS.

With the exception of the penitentiary at Deer Lodge, and the arsenal now in course of construction at the seat of government, the State has no institutions or public buildings. Provision, however, is made by Section 1 of Article 10 of the Constitution, for the establishment and support by the State, of educational, reformatory and penal institutions, and those for the benefit of the insane, blind, deaf and mute, soldier's home, and such other institutions as the public good may require.

While the establishment of these institutions is made mandatory by the Constitution, no time is fixed when Legislative action shall be taken. In view of the increase of expense to the people consequent upon a change from

Territorial to State government, and the limitation placed by the Constitution upon the public expenditures, I hope no effort will be made at this session to provide for the construction of such buildings. It might not be unwise, however, if the location of these institutions should be the subject of early consideration and settlement. The longer that it is delayed the greater will be the struggle between aspiring sections of the State for recognition in that behalf, and pending such contention, the interests of good Legislation may be subordinated if not wholly ignored. In this connection it is proper to call your attention to the fact that Legislation will be required to give force and effect to Section 2 of Article 10 of the Constitution, providing for the permanent location of the seat of government. The manner of submission, the method of canvassing the vote, and the details generally should be provided for.

FEES OF COUNTY OFFICERS.

Your attention is directed to the present fee bill of the respective county officers. The complaint is universal that the fees under the Territorial laws, and which are now injected into the State statutes, are unreasonable and excessive. While all officers should have fair and just compensation, and ought to be consulted in the establishment of fees, the citizen ought not to be compelled to surrender entirely to their demands. I recommend, therefore, a complete revision and adjustment of the present law, fixing the fees of county officers so as to make them approximately commensurate with the services rendered, and that all fees when collected be paid into the respective county treasuries, and in lieu thereof, salaries be paid to such officers.

STATE OFFICERS.

Such of the State officers as are required to reside at the seat of government, are temporarily quartered at the court house, where reasonably good accommodations are provided for most of them. No provision of law exists by which any officer is permitted to contract for the renting or leasing of offices. The County Commissioners of Lewis and Clarke county, relying upon the State to ratify the action of the occupants, have furnished and delivered the possession of offices to the following persons: The Governor, State Auditor, Chief Justice, State Treasurer, Secretary of State and Attorney General.

Many of the officers are without furniture and others are inadequately supplied. I shall have occasion to refer to these items in an estimate of the expenses of the government for the ensuing two years, which will be hereafter furnished. It becomes necessary that provision should be made for the continued occupancy of the present or other quarters of the State officers, and that the necessary contracts should be authorized and made to that end.

PUBLIC LANDS.

The act providing for our admission into the Union grants to the State public lands, which, if properly selected, managed and controlled, will place Montana second to no State in the Union in respect of educational and other

EXECUTIVE OFFICE.

institutions for which the grant was intended. It is therefore of the highest concern to the people that speedy Legislative action should be had providing for the early selection of these lands. Every day that passes lessens the value of the grant by affording opportunity for individuals to initiate settlements and rights under the land laws of the United States which will be superior to ours until the selections are made.

I call your attention to Sec. 10 of the Enabling Act, referred to, and other sections of the same act relating to the same subject. Sec. 1, Art. 18, of the Constitution seems to contemplate the creation of a board of land commissioners whose duty it shall be to classify all public lands. It appears to me that this board should be charged with the duty of making the selections provided for in Sec. 10, of the Enabling Act above referred to. I may have occasion to make this matter the subject of a separate communication hereafter, but for the present make no other recommendations concerning the same, except that in any provision you make for the sale or leasing of public lands belonging to the State, preference should be given to actual settlers, who in good faith located upon school sections by mistake, or who believing such preference would be given, have made valuable improvements upon the same.

These two classes of persons should be protected; the former for the reason of the failure of the general government to extend the public surveys, made it impossible in many cases to distinguish a school section from any other section, and the latter for the reason that the Constitution adopted and ratified by the people in 1884, contained a provision similar to the recommendation above made, and upon which numerous persons have relied and made settlements accordingly.

If, as it seems probable, the federal government shall ultimately aid in the establishment of a system of irrigation and the storage of water by means of reservoirs, no man can approximate the value of these lands to the State in the future. I make this observation to guard you against the demands of those, who, eager to monopolize our lands, will doubtless be on hand to urge a hasty and inconsiderate disposition thereof.

SALE, RENTAL AND DISTRIBUTION OF WATER.

One of the most salutary provisions in our declaration of rights, is that which makes all the water now appropriated or which may be hereafter appropriated for sale, rental, distribution or other beneficial purposes, a public use. Under this provision I assume that you are invested with ample authority to provide by appropriate legislation, against excessive and extortionate charges by individuals, companies or corporations, engaged in the sale, rental or distribution of water, and to prevent the unjust discrimination in the disposition of the same to the public. In my opinion the right of the state to regulate this subject should be asserted and maintained. I accordingly invite your attention to this matter as one worthy of your early consideration.

IRRIGATION.

Every person who is conversant with our climate and the character of our soil, must know that great possibilities await a general and comprehensive system of irrigation of our lands. I do not think the public is interested in holding a vast empire as a mere cattle range for the owners of large herds of stock. Upon the contrary, it will be a glad day for Montana when these immense herds are broken up and the stock interests of Montana shall be divided among the ranchmen in small lots. It will insure their proper feeding and shelter, and furnish employment to large numbers of persons who must also be provided with the necessaries of life, all of which will be conducive of a more general prosperity to the State. I therefore suggest that you memorialize Congress to give all possible aid to the scheme of the director of the geological survey, looking to the reclamation of our desert lands by a system of governmental irrigation by means of reservoirs, dams, etc.

CORPORATIONS.

The organization of corporations to carry on large enterprises has become a necessity in this and other states. The development of our resources, and the carrying forward of projects for the public good in many instances are of such magnitude and require an outlay of such large amounts of money that private capital cannot be induced to embark in them. The law should provide for the incorporation of such, but I condemn as bad legislation the existing statute, inherited from the Territory, which permits every character of business and industry to become the subject of an incorporation, whereby the liability of stockholders is limited. No one but a creditor is entitled to see the books of the corporation, and hence a person dealing with such concern in the first instance is at a disadvantage. I recommend the modification of existing laws so that corporations may be formed for the following and such other purposes as may be considered proper, and which shall be specifically provided for, and no other:

1. The support of public worship.
2. The support of any benevolent, charitable, educational or missionary undertaking.
3. The support of any literary or scientific undertaking, the maintenance of a library, or the promotion of painting, music, or other fine arts.
4. The encouragement of agriculture and horticulture.
5. The maintenance of public parks, and the facilities for skating and other innocent sports.
6. The maintenance of a club for social enjoyment.
7. The maintenance of a public or private cemetery.
8. The prevention and punishment of theft or of willful injury to property, and insurance against such risks.
9. The insurance of human life, and dealing in annuities.
10. The insurance of human beings against sickness or personal injuries.
11. The insurance of lives of domestic animals.
12. The insurance of property against marine risks.
13. The insurance of property against loss or injury by fire, or by any risk of inland transportation.

14. The transaction of a banking business.
15. The construction and maintenance of a railway and of a telegraph line in connection therewith.
16. The construction and maintenance of any other species of roads, and of bridges in connection therewith.
17. The construction and maintenance of a bridge.
18. The construction and maintenance of a telegraph line.
19. The establishment and maintenance of a stage line.
20. The establishment and maintenance of a ferry.
21. The building and navigation of steamboats, and carriage of persons and property thereon.
22. The supply of water to the public.
23. The manufacture and supply of gas, or the supply of light or heat to the public by other means.
24. The transaction of any manufacturing, mining, mechanical or chemical business.
25. The transaction of a printing and publishing business.
26. The establishment and maintenance of an hotel.
27. The erection of buildings and the accumulation and loan of funds for the purchase of real property.
28. The improvement of the breed of domestic animals by importation, sale or otherwise, or:
29. The construction of canals and reservoirs for conveying and storing water and the boring of artesian wells.

THE SUPREME COURT.

Under the provisions of Sec. 3, Art. 8, of the Constitution, the Supreme Court is empowered to summon a jury when required to determine an issue of fact. It will be necessary for the legislature to prescribe by law the manner in which such jury shall be summoned. There is no statute which governs this contingency.

Under the provisions of Section 4 of the same article the Legislative Assembly should fix the time for holding the terms of the Supreme Court, or confer the authority upon the justices to regulate them. I think the number of terms should be increased to four, and that the assembly should designate them. This legislation would secure a speedy hearing of appeals and render certain the day when they could be heard.

CLERK OF THE SUPREME COURT.

The Constitution has deemed the office of Clerk of the Supreme Court of such importance, that it has required him to be elected by the votes of the people of the State. The fees alowed for his services should be revised, and when collected paid into the treasury. This officer should receive a salary.

CODE COMMISSION.

The important work of preparing the four codes authorized by the act of

March 14, 1889, was committed to a commission which was required to report three of the codes to the next ensuing Legislature. The commission has been industriously engaged in the work since the adoption of the State Constitution, and has completed and filed with the Secretary of State the "civil code." I am in receipt of a communication from the chairman of the commission under date of November 13, 1889, from which the following extract is made:

"The commission found it impossible to commence the work contemplated by the act creating it, until after the formation of the State Constitution which was completed on the 17th day of August, 1889. Soon after that day the commission commenced its labors and has worked continuously ever since that time with the following result: We have completed and filed with the Secretary of State "the civil code" which occupied all of our time every day for nearly three months. We find the work of such a character that it cannot be hurried and well done. The code already completed might be improved if we had more time to bestow upon it, but the act creating the commission requires three of the codes to be submitted to the next Legislature. Probably it was in the contemplation of the Legislature that authorized the creation of the code commission that the next legislature would not meet for two years, thus giving the commission two years to perform its labors. At any rate we find it impossible to complete three of the codes in time to submit to the Legislature which is called to meet on November 23, 1889. It appears to us that the four codes authorized by the act aforesaid, should all be submitted to the Legislature at the same time. Necessarily each of the codes contain sections and provisions that refer to each other, and unless all the codes go into effect at the same time, many of the sections and provisions will be inoperative and void.

The Constitution has not only provided an entirely new system of courts for civil business, but has made a radical change in the manner of prosecuting criminal cases, and the commission finds that much time and labor will be required to formulate the necessary statutes by which changes made by the Constitution can be put in operation and carried into effect.

We therefore suggest that the commission be given further time in which to complete its work."

While it is desirable that this work shall be completed at the earliest practicable time, every consideration of public policy dictates that sufficient time should be given to insure such thoroughness as will be a guarantee that the work when completed will be well done. I accordingly concur in the suggestion of the chairman of the code commission above referred to, and recommend that such further time be given to report as may be deemed necessary.

LABOR.

Provision is made in the Constitution for a bureau of labor and industry, to be located at the capital, and to be under the control of a commissioner to be appointed by the Governor, and subject to confirmation by the Senate. I regard the creation of this office as of the greatest importance to the State. It

EXECUTIVE OFFICE. 15

will be the medium through which can be collected and preserved authentic statistics and information generally of great value in the adjustment and perfection of future legislation. While our population is small and our industries comparatively few, the salary should be moderate.

PUBLIC EXAMINER.

Section 8 of Article 7 of the Constitution makes it your duty to provide for a state examiner, and in addition to the duties specifically enjoined upon that official by the Constitution, he is required to perform such other duties as the Legislature may prescribe. His compensation should be fixed by law.

BOARD OF PARDONS.

The Constitution has provided for a board of pardons to consist of the Governor, Secretary of State and Attorney General. Before the power to pardon can be exercised, the Legislative Assembly must provide the time and place of meeting of the board, and regulate generally its procedure.

A large number of applications were pending at the time I qualified as Governor, and several have been filed since that time. I have directed your attention specially to this subject with the hope that appropriate legislation may be speedily enacted.

HOMESTEAD AND EXEMPTIONS.

Homestead and exemption laws are the outgrowth of civilization, and in all enlightened communities there is a universal concurrence of sentiment in favor of making them broad and liberal. Society owes something to the wife and children and the creditor who trusts the reckless and improvident, ought not to be permitted to pursue the former to destitution. I therefore recommend that in obedience to the Constitution. liberal homestead and exemption laws be enacted.

REGISTRATION.

The Constitution gives the Legislature power to enact suitable registration laws.

The schedule annexed to the Constitution provides for the continuing in force all laws of the Territory not inconsistent with the Constitution, or the Constitution and laws of the United States. By this the registration law enacted by the last Territorial Legislature becomes a part of our State statutes. While the Legislature ought to throw around the ballot every safeguard against fraud and repeating, and a proper registration law is conducive to this end, the present system overshoots the mark and operates to disfranchise many good citizens of this State whose votes are entitled to be cast and counted. In my opinion no registration should be required as a condition precedent to voting in remote and sparsely settled communities. The facilities for transportation are inadequate in such sections of the country, and those afforded are expensive and often beyond the means of voters. Mountain ranges are sometimes required to be crossed, and the distance required to be traveled has been shown to be in some instances as much as a hundred miles, and not infrequently from twelve to twenty miles. The result of this is that the ranchmen, the stock herder and the prospector, who form a large per cent. of our population, and who are generally impecunious and unable to bear the burden of such an expense and loss of time as the present system necessarily entails, are compelled to remain at home, and are thereby disfranchised on election day. To obviate this wrong done to the citizen, I recommend that the present registration law be so amended that registration shall not be required except in incorporated cities, or towns having a given population. It is in the latter places, the centres of population, where lawbreakers and malefactors congregate, and repenting and fraud are practiced, and not in remote precincts where every man knows his neighbor and a stranger is at once observed. I believe that it is an undue and unnecessary burden on the citizen to require him to register every time there is a general election. Having once registered that ought to be sufficient for at least six years. I therefore recommend such modification of existing laws as will remedy this evil.

PURITY OF THE BALLOT.

The last Territorial Legislature inaugurated a ballot reform that is worthy of note. While the Australian system of voting, as a whole, does not come up to public expectation, it is, nevertheless, a departure in the right direction, and its general acceptance by the people, with some modifications, is in my opinion assured. There should be no abatement of public interest in legislation designed to secure and perpetuate the purity of the ballot. The present law would be just as effective as it was designed to be if, instead of printing the names of all the candidates on one continuous ticket, their names were placed in parallel columns representing the party whose political principles they avowed. I recommend this modification of the law. The present system is tantamount to an educational qualification on the one hand, or a complete surrender upon the other to judges of election, who, in many cases, are incompetent and in some cases venal. The time is too short to point out the many imperfections of a law which was well intended, but which to the most casual observer, in the light of observation and actual experience, has been demonstrated to be very crude. If this system can be simplified and at the same time preserve its essential qualities, in my opinion, it will popularize politics and in the end secure the most perfect reflection of the popular will of any system ever inaugurated. It stimulates courage in the dependent to vote according to his conscientious convictions, and above all, it strikes savagely at the method of machine politics and promises its complete annihilation. In other words, simplified and properly guarded, it secures to the voter the largest freedom of thought, independence of action and exercise of judgment of any system which has ever obtained to my knowledge.

If our institutions are to endure, and the honor, integrity and prosperity of the State are to continue to be the hope and anchor of the citizen, the voice of the people, expressed at the polls without hinderance or intimidation, must be sedulously guarded and maintained at all hazards. The duty of the officers charged with the responsibility of declaring the result of an election should be so explicit, and the punishment for misconduct made so severe that the temptation for venal treachery at vital points will be forever removed. I call your attention to the unusual and unnecessary expense in the matter of printing, which the present election law entails upon the people. It should be framed to meet only necessary and proper expenses.

CONSTITUTIONAL AMENDMENT.

Conscious of the fact that the Constitutional Convention which formulated and adopted our Constitution committed a grievous mistake in providing for the apportionment and representation of Senators, by which population, the only just basis of representation under our form of government, was wholly ignored, I call upon the Legislative Assembly at the first opportunity to provide for the early submission of a Constitutional amendment whereby this inequality may be speedily corrected.

INDIAN RESERVATIONS.

The large Indian reservations within our borders which were set aside by the general government, embrace some of our best agricultural lands, and are far in excess of the requirements of the Indians, who are no longer able or compelled to live by the chase, but in every instance are the recipients of bounties from the government. The buffalo and wild game which once abounded upon these reservations are practically extinct, and with their departure disappeared the only reason for the maintenance of large areas of land for the occupancy of the Indians.

I therefore hope that you will memorialize Congress to compel a speedy selection and acceptance of these lands by individual members of Indian tribes, and for an early restoration of the remainder to the public domain.

EXPENSES OF CONSTITUTIONAL CONVENTION.

The twenty thousand dollars appropriated by Congress to defray the expenses of holding the late Constitutional Convention, was found to be inadequate for that purpose. Additional clerk hire and other officers, including a stenographer, and a stenographic report of the proceedings of the Convention was, by resolution of the Convention, declared to be necessary and proper for the convenient and early dispatch of its business. To cover these extra expenses, the Convention adopted an ordinance appropriating the following sums for the following purposes respectively, and declared the same to be charges against the State of Montana:

The item for the stenographic report is an approximation, but of course is capable of being rendered certain when the report is filed.

John Trumbull, clerk .... $ 220
E. C. Garrett, clerk 215

John McCay, clerk	220
Lee Swords, clerk	215
Edward Kerr, clerk	215
Henry Bernard, clerk	215
Miss Jennie Merriam, clerk	160
William Taylor, clerk	55
William Green, Assistant Sergeant at Arms	175
Morris Langhorne, page	172
Cornelius Hedges, page	172
Wm. D. Alexander, page	172
Henry Bernard, for supervising the printing of the Constitution and type writing	100
Lee Swords, for acting as clerk of committee on address	25
C. P. Connolly, stenographer	675
C. P. Connolly, transcript of proceedings and debates of Constitutional Convention (estimated)	3,500
Printing 20,000 copies of the Constitution (estimated)	2,100
Total	$8,606

I therefore recommend that the same be paid by the State and that Congress be memorialized to reimburse the State, as it intended by its enabling act to cover all expenses of the Convention. In as much as this ordinance was not submitted to the people for ratification and by them ratified, legislation is required to give it effect.

THE COURT IN SILVER BOW COUNTY.

The most unseemly condition of affairs exists in Silver Bow County. Two persons are assuming to act as judges of the district court in that county. One has behind him the decision of a court of competent jurisdiction, establishing his right to the office, the other has the certificate of the late governor of the Territory. Pending this controversy, litigants are without the tribunals for the settlement of their grievances, the estates of deceased persons are jeopardised, business generally is in a state of suspended animation, and the courts are brought into contempt. The case in which the rights of the respective claimants are involved is now on appeal to the supreme court, it having been decided that no stay of proceedings was allowed. From what has been said heretofore you will observe that I assume that legislation is required fixing the terms of the supreme court before that case can be ultimately disposed of. This situation of affairs is of serious concern to the citizens of Silver Bow county in particular, and to the people of the entire State in general, and I may add that it is, or ought to be, humiliating to the pride of every citizen of this State. I recommend that provision be made for holding a term of the supreme court at the earliest practicable time, in order that this matter may be speedily and finally determined.

The power committed to your hands involves a sacred trust. The manner in which it is exercised will invite public approval or condemnation. At no time since our Territorial organization has there been such a large number of citizens who vote independently of past party affiliations. The judgment of these is stern and severe ; a wise exercise, therefore, of this power by the executive and legislative branches of the government will invite public confidence, and furnish cause for congratulation upon our assumption of the new and well-fitting dignity of Statehood.

Whenever, for supposed political advantages, the honor, the welfare and the glory of the State is prostituted to partisan ends, the inevitable penalty will be the destruction of popular confidence and disaster at the polls.

DUAL HOUSE OF REPRESENTATIVES.

Two bodies are now sitting, each claiming to be the legal House of Representatives; one assembled and is sitting in the place designated by the Executive for that purpose, the other assembled in a place designated by the State Auditor, and is now sitting in another place of its own choosing. This condition of affairs has prevailed for more than three weeks. It is born of impulse. Passion has had time to cool and returning reason ought to assert itself. It is high time that personal ambitions should be subordinated to patriotism and the wheels of government be permitted to roll. It is to be regretted that the body wrongfully assuming to be the House of Representatives, and which met in the place designated by the Auditor, misinterpreted the proclamation of the Executive, as well as the letter of instruction to Captain Smith, as claimed by the report adopted and promulgated by its committee. Fully appreciating the wise distinction between the Executive and the legislative departments of the government, and the independence of each as contemplated by the Constitution, and desiring to be fairly considered by my countrymen, honor bids me forget pride and will not permit me to conclude this message without putting on perpetual record a solemn and public refutation of the charge "that the Governor, by his proclamation or otherwise, at the time it was issued, or at any other time, ever intended to interfere with the right of any person claiming to be a member of the House of Representatives to his seat," or, "that it was the intention of the Governor to conceal the said instructions to the said John Smith, until after the temporary organization of the House of Representatives and by virtue of his control of the room in which the people's representatives were to assemble, to dictate who would enter therein."

While the Constitution provides: "That the supreme executive power of the State shall be vested in the Governor, who shall see that the laws are faithfully executed," no authority was ever assumed except to "declare the law," in the hope that those persons who had the proper certificates of election would advise those who did not to refrain from participation in the organization of the House. The facts disclosed in the proclamation justified the Executive at that time in the hope that such a course would be pursued, but no intimation was ever given that force would be employed to that end. In the light of the past it is possible that the language of the proclamation may have led some honest men to believe that the Executive was wrongfully encroaching upon the legislative branch of the government, but conscious of the fact that no such purpose was intended, I call upon those recalcitrant members who claim to have been misled by the Governor, to stand not upon a matter of punctillio in the presence of such threatening danger to the State, but to join with their colleagues in the transaction of the public business.

Of course there can be but one legal House of Representatives. No legislation can be had until that point is settled and acquiesced in by the Senate and the Executive. Let us hope that your wisdom may provide a speedy and satisfactory solution of the pending difficulties. Every consideration demands an amicable adjustment, if such a thing is possible, and I earnestly hope for such a result. But important as this session has been shown to be, it is better that it should lapse and all legislation fail, than that the principles upon which our government is founded should be treated as a mere commodity to be exchanged ad libitum to promote the aspirations of men for office. I therefore hope that in all your negotiations looking to the settlement of this perplexing question, you will have an "eye single and a warm, devoted heart" for what in your best judgment you consider to be the true interest of your country. When this is done, our efforts to serve the State wisely and well will be crowned with success; the burthens of taxation will, let us hope, be mitigated; justice will be peacefully enthroned in the temple now claimed by contending judges; the fruition of our hope of statehood will, in a measure, be enjoyed, and government will be felt, if at all, most in its benefits and least in its restraints.
JOS. K. TOOLE.
GOVERNOR.

Executive Office, Helena, Mont., Dec. 17, 1889.

Message to the Second Legislative Assembly of the State of Montana.

GENTLEMEN OF THE LEGISLATIVE ASSEMBLY:

Obedient to that provision of the Constitution which requires me, at the beginning of each session, to give to the Legislative Assembly information of the condition of the State, and to make such recommendation as deemed expedient, I have the honor to submit for your consideration the following message.

The year which has just closed finds us in a flourishing condition. Mining, stock raising and agriculture, the three principal industries in which we are conspicuously successful, have made rapid strides in development. Great irrigating enterprises are on foot by which our fertile soil will be made to respond in a greatly increased measure. Our oft asserted claim for the capacity of our soil to produce the best and most prolific yield of wheat, oats and barley, has been fully established and maintained.

Our great and diversified resources, by which we are self-supporting,

EXECUTIVE OFFICE.   21

have made us virtually independent of the financial stress which has lately oppressed with disastrous effects less favored communities.

A brief reference to official data furnished this office justifies the following comparative statement:

A year ago our total assessment was	$ 79,376,944
Now it is (see exhibit "A")	112,457,555
A year ago our mineral output was	24,012,000
Now it is	47,848,000
A year ago the number horses, sheep and cattle in Montana was	1,881,268
Now it is	2,368,482
A year ago the number of bushels of wheat, oats and barley produced was	2,648,149
Now it is	4,111,907
A year ago the number of pounds of wool produced was	7,023,134
Now it is	7,784,007
A year ago the number of quartz mills and reduction furnaces operated was	188
Now it is	207
A year ago the number of bushels of coal mined was	907,500
Now it is (629,200) tons	17,612,000
A year ago the number of miles of completed railroad was	2,043
Now we have	2,365
A year ago we collected in revenue from all sources	$149,316 70
This year we collected	309,429 23
We have paid out since November 8, 1889	193,437 99
Unpaid claims against the State requiring appropriations (approximated)	167,819 95
Money in treasury December 31, 1890	187,181 49

A table showing net indebtedness of the several counties up to March 1, 1890, and increase or decrease for the year ending February 28, 1890, is hereto appended, marked "Exhibit B," also a table showing the condition of the several funds, and the amounts contributed to each by the several counties is marked "Exhibit C."

This remarkable march of progress, when augmented by federal legislation looking to the reclamation of our arid lands and the increase of the circulating medium which will follow the free and unlimited coinage of silver, will reach a point far beyond the expectations of the most sanguine.

But our great resources and almost limitless possibilities should not tempt us into improvident expenditures of the people's money. Against this the Constitution stands as an insuperable barrier. Section 12, article 12, of the Constitution is important at the outset.

"Sec. 12. No appropriation shall be made or any expenditures authorized by the Legislative Assembly whereby the expenditures of the State during any fiscal year shall exceed the total tax then provided for by law, and applicable to such appropriation or expenditure, unless the Legislative Assembly making such appropriation shall provide for levying a sufficient tax, not exceeding the rate allowed in section 9 of this article, to pay such appropriations or expenditures within such fiscal year. This provision shall not apply to appropriations or expenditures to suppress insurrection, defend the State, or assist in defending the United States in time of war. No appropriation of public moneys shall be made for a longer term than two years."

Considerable difficulty has at times been experienced in carrying on the necessary affairs of State which will be spoken of hereafter under appropriate headings. This has resulted from the want of the necessary legislation to put Constitutional provisions into effect and to meet many new conditions which have arisen on account of the change from Territorial to State government, but upon the whole we have succeeded fairly well. The prospect for the future is inviting, and the wholesome restraints of our Constitution above referred to are safe guarantees against incurring indebtedness beyond our ability to pay.

STATE LEVY.

One of the first acts which you will be called upon to perform will be under section 1, article 12, of the Constitution, requiring you to "levy a uniform rate of assessment and taxation." Section 9 of the same article is as follows:

"Sec. 9. The rate of taxation of real and personal property for State purposes, in any one year, shall never exceed three (3) mills on each dollar of valuation; and whenever the taxable property in the State shall amount to one hundred million dollars ($100,000,000), the rate shall not exceed two and one-half mills on each dollar of valuation; and whenever the taxable property in the State shall amount to three hundred million dollars ($300,000,000), the rate shall not exceed one and one-half mills on each dollar of valuation; unless a proposition to increase such rate, specifying the rate proposed and the time during which the same shall be levied, shall have been submitted to the people at a general election, and shall have received a majority of all the votes cast for and against it at such election."

Our demands will require the largest levy permissable under the Constitution, to-wit, two and one-half mills.

THE PENITENTIARY.

The penitentiary, formerly belonging to and under control of the United States, has now become the property of the State. The same, with the lands connected therewith, were granted to the State by the act providing for our admission into the Union. Under our Territorial organization, the control and management of this institution was under the exclusive jurisdiction of the United States, with whom the Territory contracted for the maintenance and support of its prisoners. In providing for the change from Territorial to State government, no provision was made to cover the period between the date of admission and the time when the Legislature should provide for the proper management of the same. Between that date, however, and the 1st day of March, 1890, the United States marshal remained in charge, under the contract between the Territory and the United States. On the latter date I found the United States no longer willing to continue in charge. I accordingly contracted with Mr. Frank Conley and Thomas McTague, of Deer Lodge City, Montana,

EXECUTIVE OFFICE. 23

for the care, custody and maintenance of the institution and inmates (subject to the ratification of the Legislative Assembly), at the rate of seventy cents per day per capita for all over one hundred, and sixty-five cents per capita for all over two hundred.

The price paid the United States by the Territory was eighty-five cents per capita. The performance of this contract was secured by a bond of $50,000. The contractors have, I believe, faithfully performed their part of the contract. They have trusted entirely to the good faith and ability of the State to reimburse them, and I earnestly hope this may be done without delay. Independent of the value of improvements made by the contractors, for which reasonable compensation should be made, there is now due them the sum of $44,-901.90.

How shall the prison be managed in the future? Shall a Warden be appointed and appropriations made direct to maintain it under State control and Supervision, or will the contract system be continued? These are questions submitted to your sound judgment.

So far as the mere cost to the State is concerned, I am inclined to believe that the contract system, under such rules and regulations as the Board of Prison Managers might make, would be more advantageous to the State. Whatever conclusion is reached in that connection, it is absolutely necessary that considerable improvements should be made in the prison and the grounds.

The dictates of humanity and a decent regard for the health and possible reformation of the inmates demand more commodious quarters and such an arrangement that young offenders may not be compelled to be incarcerated with the chronic and more vicious criminals. The capacity of the penitentiary is about one hundred and forty men. Whole number confined January 1, 1891, 240. During the year past seventy-nine were released, two by pardon, seventy by expiration of sentence, two delivered for new trials and five by death. Of the number confined to December, 1890, the sex and color were as follows:

```
White males.......................................217
White females....................................  8
Colored males....................................  6
Colered females..................................  1
Indians..........................................  8
Chinese..........................................  7
                                                 ----
Total............................................247
```

The crimes for which they were convicted embrace: murder, robbery, attempted rape, assault with deadly weapon, assault to do bodily harm, assault to commit burglary, burglary, breaking jail, crime against nature, embezzlement, forgery, larceny, manslaughter, assault to commit murder, obtaining valuable papers under false pretences, obtaining money under false pretences, perjury, resisting officer, receiving stolen property, assault to commit robbery, sodomy, and the terms of punishment range from one year to life. Of the latter there are sixteen; one hundred and eighty-four were citizens of the United States, and fifty-eight were foreigners. Counties sent from:

Beaverhead	13
Cascade	12
Choteau	19
Custer	11
Deer Lodge	24
Dawson	2
Fergus	9
Gallatin	9
Jefferson	5
Lewis and Clarke	40
Madison	3
Meagher	5
Missoula	19
Park	17
Silver Bow	47
Yellowstone	7
Total	247

The first annual report of the contractors will be hereafter placed before you.

INSANE.

The insane of the State are supported under contract between the Territory of Montana and Doctors Mitchell and Mussigbrod, at Warm Springs, Deer Lodge County, Montana, at $8 per week, making an expense to the State of about $75,000 per annum. The number is increasing rapidly, the last report showing two hundred patients maintained at public expense. The maintenance of the insane and the penitentiary will form the largest items of pexense under our State government. The proper treatment of those unfortunates committed to the asylum, at the least possible expense to the State, calls for the exercise of your best judgment. I am not prepared at this time to say that any new arrangement would be advantageous to the State, or to the persons confined therein, but in view of the great and growing expense in that behalf, I urge the most thorough investigation of the subject. The contractors have received nothing from the State, in payment under their contract, since January 8, 1890. There is consequently due them the sum of $77,380.61. This looks like a great hardship to impose upon the contractors, who claim to be paying interest upon the amount in order to maintain this institution. The situation calls for prompt action. I invite attention to the annual report of the contractors in this connection which will be hereafter transmitted.

OTHER UNFORTUNATES SUPPORTED BY THE STATE.

The State is now supporting and educating five deaf and dumb children at public institutes. Three at Washington, D. C., one at Danville, Ky., and one at Baltimore, Md.; also one blind child at Nashville, Tenn. We also support five feeble minded children; two of the latter are at Binghampton, N. Y., and three at Elwin. Pa. Each of the children is costing the State an average of $300 per annum, besides transportation going and returning.

Of this number two have been sent within the past year. Contracts for their keeping have been entered into for from one to six years, according to the age of the child. These facts are submitted in the hope that they may become the basis for intelligent consideration of the claims which these unfortunates have upon the State and humanity.

STATE INSTITUTIONS AND PUBLIC BUILDINGS.

I have already referred to the penitentiary at Deer Lodge. Aside from this there is no other public building belonging to the State except the armory at the State Capital. On the 22d day of October, A. D., 1889, Hon. B. F. White, late Governor of Montana Territory, entered into a contract with one A. McCarter for the erection of a State Armory for the contract price of $13,300, besides such extra work as the contractors and architects might agree upon. The work was not completed at the time of the change from the Territorial to the State government. Work, however, continued and the building was completed and is now occupied for the purpose intended. Its completion found us in debt to the contractors on account of balance due in the sum of $5,591.75.

There is no authority of law to pay it out of money in the State treasury. The demand for the building was as urgent as the demand by the contractor for his money. A number of the public-spirited gentlemen of the Capital came to the rescue, endorsed the note of the State officers upon which the Cruse Savings Bank of Helena advanced the money to pay off the contractor. This note, with the interest is still due and will be brought to your attention in connection with other unpaid claims against the State.

In connection with the use of the building as an armory the same is occupied by several companies of the National Guard of Montana under an arrangement by which each company is to pay an annual rental of $300 out of the money allowed by law to the several companies, but which in the absence of necessary legislation they have been unable to draw. The building has been insured in three companies for the sum of $15,000. There was no money available to pay this and the several agents of these companies are generously carrying the State for the premiums pending authority to pay the same. The companies of the National Guard in Helena have, by their combined efforts, raised several hundred dollars which have been expended in necessary work to make the building inhabitable. Upon the whole I may add that public generosity has been taxed to the utmost to utilize the armory, all of which has been made necessary on account of a failure to properly provide by legislation for its completion and maintenance.

OTHER BUILDINGS.

Provision is made by Section 1, of Article 10, of the Constitution, for the establishment and support by the State of educational, reformatory and penal institutions, and those for the benefit of the insane, blind, deaf and dumb, soldiers' home and such other institutions as the public good may require.

While the establishment of these institutions is made mandatory by the Constitution, no time is fixed when legislative action shall be taken. In view of the limitation placed by the Constitution upon the public expenditure I hope no effort will be made at this session to provide for the construction of such buildings. It would be wise, however, if the location of these institutions should be the subject of early consideration and settlement. The longer that is delayed the greater will be the struggle between aspiring sections of the State for recognition in that behalf, and pending such contention, the interests of good legislation may be subordinated if not wholly ignored. In this connection it is proper to call your attention to the fact that legislation will be required to give force to Section 2, of Article 10, of the Constitution, providing for the permanent location of the seat of government; the manner of submission, the manner of canvassing the votes and the details generally should be provided for.

STATE MILITIA.

Section 3, Article 14, of the Constitution, makes it incumbent upon the State to maintain the militia by appropriations from the State treasury. In view of this provision it becomes a question of great concern how to maintain this organization so as to preserve its efficiency in case of danger and at the same time reduce the expense to the minimum. All extraordinary and unnecessary expenses should be discontinued and eliminated from the law. It is obvious that with the many demands made upon the State treasury, consequent upon a change of government, the practice of the most rigid economy in every department is imperative. In appropriating money for this as well as all other institutions of the State, we must keep constantly in view that provision of the Constitution prohibiting the passage of an appropriation or the issuance of any warrant beyond the amount raised by taxation. In other words our Constitution was framed upon the principle of administering our affairs upon a cash basis, except when the proposition to raise a tax is submitted to the people at a general election. Our revenue will be insufficient to maintain a militia upon the scale provided in the present military code. It is claimed by many that one half of the number of companies properly disciplined and well provided for would be more serviceable and creditable to the State than the entire militia as now organized. It is also claimed that the annual encampment now provided for might be well abandoned without detriment to the service and a system of inspection instituted in lieu thereof.

These items alone would result in a saving of about $20,000 per annum.

Upon these questions there is a difference of opinion among the staff, regimental and other officers of the National Guard, but all who have expressed an opinion agree that expenses should be reduced. I accordingly recommend an organization upon a less expensive plan until the resources of the State will justify a more comprehensive one. I think the Governor should have authority to issue arms to settlers in remote places in case of threatened danger. It cannot be done now without making himself personally responsible for loss of property.

EXECUTIVE OFFICE.

STATE OFFICERS.

Such of the State officers as are required to reside at the seat of government are quartered at the court house, where reasonably good accommodations are provided for most of them. No provision of law exists by which any officer is permitted to contract for the renting or leasing of offices. The County Commissioners of Lewis and Clarke county, relying upon the State to ratify the actions of the occupants, have furnished and delivered the possession of offices to the following persons: Governor, Secretary of State, Auditor, Treasurer, Attorney General, Superintendent of Public Instruction and Judges of the Supreme Court. So far as I am informed the quarters furnished are well adapted to such uses and reasonably satisfactory. We have paid no rent to the county, although we have occupied the rooms for more than a year. I recommend that authority be given some officer of this State to enter into a proper contract for quarters and that provision be made to pay the same.

Your attention is also called to the fact that there is no law in existence by which the vote for State officers to be elected in 1892 can be canvassed or the result of the election declared.

The State Constitution provided the method of giving effect to the first election only. The necessity of legislation upon this question is urgent. The term of office of the present incumbents expires on the first day of January, 1893, and does not continue, as is usual, until their successors are elected and qualified.

REPORTS OF STATE OFFICERS.

Section 19, of Article 7, of the Constitution requires all State officers to make a full and complete report of their official transactions to the Governor at least twenty days preceding each regular session of the Legislative Assembly, which report is thereafter to be transmitted to the legislature by the Governor. In order to make this report available and of practical value so far as the financial condition of the State is concerned, it will be necessary to change the present law and make all taxes delinquent after the 30th day of November instead of December 31st and I recommend the change, and I further recommend as a matter of convenience and economy that all reports of State officers required to be printed, be printed in one volume.

GREAT SEAL OF THE STATE.

We are still using the old seal of the Territory. A State seal should be adopted. Also a seal for the Supreme Court.

STATE BOARD OF EQUALIZATION.

The creation of this board is a radical departure from former methods in this State.

Sections 15, 16 and 18, of Article 12, of the Constitution are as follows:

Sec. 15. The Governor, Secretary of State, State Treasurer, State Auditor and Attorney General shall constitute a State Board of Equalization and the

Board of County Commissioners of each county shall constitute a County Board of Equalization. The duty of the State Board of Equalization shall be to adjust and Equalize the valuation of the taxable property among the several counties of the State. The duty of the County Board of Equalization shall be to adjust and equalize the valuation of the taxable property within their respective counties. Each Board shall also perform such other duties as may be prescribed by law.

Sec. 16. All property shall be assessed in the manner prescribed by law except as is otherwise provided in this Constitution. The franchise, roadway, roadbed, rails and rolling stock of all railroads operated in more than one county in this State shall be assessed by the State Board of Equalization and the same shall be apportioned to the counties, cities, towns, townships and school districts in which such railroads are located in proportion to the number of miles of railway laid in such counties, cities, towns, townships and school districts.

Sec. 18. The Legislative Assembly shall pass laws necessary to carry out the provisions of this article.

Pursuant to these provisions the Board organized and proceeded to a discharge of its duties. An examination of the authorities soon satisfied the Board that the foregoing provisions were inoperative without the necessary legislation. It proceeded, however, basing its action in nearly every instance upon an agreement with the railroad companies by which the assessments were made and the taxes paid.

The labor involved in securing the necessary information, preparing the proper blanks, together with travel, conference and correspondence has been great; and all done and performed under great difficulties.

The whole subject has been thoroughly considered and legislation recommended by the Board of Equalization in its first annual report which has been printed and which will be hereafter submitted. I will not, therefore, encumber this message with them but fully endorse the report and recommend the legislation proposed as proper and necessary.

BOARD OF PARDONS.

The Constitution has provided for a Board of Pardons consisting of the Secretary of State, State Auditor, and Attorney General.

No legislation has ever been enacted providing for the time or place of its meetings or defining its procedure in any respect.

The Board, however, deeming it had sufficient authority so to do, organized and have proceeded to act upon various cases passed on by the executive, making its own rules, etc., etc. These rules or similar ones should be enacted as law or direct authority conferred upon the Board to make the same.

During the year twenty-nine applications for pardon were presented to me. Out of this number twenty-two were rejected by me; five were granted and two commuted. These latter cases went before the Board of Pardons for its action, which resulted in the approval of five and disapproval of two.

The report of the Board showing its organization, rules of procedure, cases considered and other information in detail will be hereafter presented.

The present system of pardons is a radical departure from that which has existed since our organization as a Territory; yet nothing has come under my observation to subject it to criticism.

STATE BOARD OF EDUCATION.

Section 11, Article 11, of the Constitution, is as follows:

Sec. 11. The general control and supervision of the State University and the various other State educational institutions shall be vested in a State Board of Education, whose powers and duties shall be prescribed and regulated by law. The said Board shall consist of eleven members, the Governor, State Superintendent of Public Instruction and Attorney General being members ex-officio; the other eight members thereof shall be appointed by the Governor, subject to the confirmation of the Senate, under the regulations and restrictions to be provided by law.

This section evidently contemplates that legislation shall be passed defining the term of office, qualification, etc., of the Board. I would suggest that in formulating the law provision should be made for the expiration of one term every year, which would secure the service of experienced men at all times on the Board.

STATE BOARD OF EXAMINERS AND PRISON COMMISSIONERS.

Section 20, Article 7, of the Constitution, is as follows:

Sec. 20. The Governor, Secretary of State and Attorney General shall constitute a Board of State Prison Commissioners, which Board shall have such supervision of all matters connected with the State prisons as may be prescribed by law. They shall constitute a Board of Examiners with power to examine all claims against the State, except salaries or compensation of officers fixed by law, and perform such other duties as may be prescribed by law. And no claim against the State except for salaries and compensation of officers as fixed by law, shall be passed upon by the Legislative Assembly without first having been considered and acted upon by said Board.

The powers, procedure and duties of the Board should be prescribed by law. The numerous claims filed against the State have not been examined or passed upon by the Board of Examiners, nor has anything been done by the Board of Prison Commissioners except to organize, visit and inspect the Penitentiary with a view of ascertaining the manner in which it was conducted and what additions and repairs should be made thereto. A separate report upon that proposition will be hereafter submitted.

LABOR.

Provision is made in the Constitution for a Bureau of Labor and Industry, to be located at the Capital, and to be under the control of a commissioner to be appointed by the Governor, and subject to confirmation by the Senate. I regard the creation of this office as of the greatest importance to the State.

It will be the medium through which can be collected and preserved authentic statistics and information generally of great value in the adjustment and perfection of future legislation. While our population is small and our industries comparatively few, the salary should be moderate.

PUBLIC EXAMINER.

Section 8, Article 7, of the Constitution makes it your duty to provide for a State Examiner, and in addition to the duties specifically enjoined upon that official by the Constitution, he is required to perform such other duties as the Legislature may prescribe. His compensation should be fixed by law.

APPORTIONMENT AND REPRESENTATION.

Section 2, Article 6, of the Constitution provides as follows:

Sec. 2. The Legislative Assembly shall provide by law for an enumeration of the inhabitants of the State in the year 1885 and every tenth year thereafter; and at the session next following an enumeration made by the authority of the United States, shall revise and adjust the apportionment for representatives on the basis of such enumeration according to the ratios to be fixed by law. From this it appears that the present Legislature will be called upon to revise and adjust the apportionment for Representatives, and in so doing they are required to take as a basis the enumeration last made by the United States, an enumeration, which, so far as this State is concerned, was a complete and elaborate failure. It will furnish the basis for an unjust apportionment which must be tolerated until after 1895, when an enumeration may be made by the State as provided by Section 2, above referred to, if legislation to that end is enacted.

COMPENSATION OF MEMBERS OF THE LEGISLATURE.

In view of the fact that the Constitution has declared that the compensation of the Legislative Assembly after the first shall be as provided by law, and that no Legislative Assembly shall fix its own compensation, it will be incumbent on you to give this subject attention at this session.

PUBLIC LANDS.

The act providing for our admission into the Union grants to the State public lands, which, if properly selected, managed and controlled, will place Montana second to no State in the Union in respect of educational and other institutions for which the grant was intended. It is therefore of the highest concern to the people that speedy legislative action should be had providing for the early selection of these lands. Every day that passes lessens the value of the grant by affording opportunity for individuals to initiate settlements and rights under the land laws of the United States which will be superior to ours until the selections are made. In this connection we should not be unmindful of the fact that suits are pending and legislation is being urged for the purpose of dispossessing the Northern Pacific Railroad Company of thousands of acres of mineral land within this State claimed under its grant,

EXECUTIVE OFFICE.

and that for every acre so taken it will claim an equivalent of agricultural land. A bare suggestion of this subject is sufficient to stimulate our efforts in securing an early selection of the land granted to the State, otherwise the gift of the Government may not be worth the taking. I call your attention to Section 10 of the enabling act referred to, and other sections of the same act relating to the same subject. Section 1, Article 18, of the Constitution seems to contemplate the creation of a Board of Land Commissioners, whose duty it shall be to classify all public lands. It appears to me that this board should be charged with the duty of making the selections provided for in Section 10 of the enabling act above referred to. In any provision you make for the sale or leasing of public lands belonging to the State, preference should be given to actual settlers, who in good faith located upon school sections by mistake, or who believing such preference would be given, have made valuable improvements upon the same.

These two classes of persons should be protected: the former for the reason that the failure of the general government to extend the public surveys, made it impossible in many instances to distinguish a school section from any other section, and the other for the reason that the Constitution adopted and ratified by the people in 1884, contained a provision similar to the recommendation above made, and upon which numerous persons have relied and made settlements accordingly.

If the federal government or the State shall ultimately aid in the establishment of a system of irrigation and the storage of water by means of reservoirs, no man can approximate the value of these lands to the State in the future. I make this observation to guard you against the demands of those who, eager to monopolize our lands, will doubtless be on hand to urge a hasty and inconsiderate disposition thereof.

Section 13 of the enabling act provides:

Sec. 13. That five per centum of the proceeds of the sale of public lands lying within said States which shall be sold by the United States subsequent to the admission of said States into the Union, after deducting all the expenses incident to the same shall be paid to the States, to be used as a permanent fund, the interest of which only shall be expended for the support of the common schools within said States respectively.

This fund, whatever it may be, should be placed to our credit so that it may be invested and return some revenue to the State. Legislation to authorize its investment must, however, be first provided.

Congress has been well disposed in advancing educational interests, and it remains for us to avail ourselves of its munificence.

AGRICULTURAL COLLEGE.

By an act of Congress approved August 30, 1890, $15,000 per annum and an increase of $1,009 per annum for the period of ten years thereafter is appropriated to each State and Territory, and after that the sum of $25,000 per annum to be applied only to instruction in agriculture, the mechanic arts, the

English language and the various branches of mathematical, physical, natural and economic science. In order to avail ourselves of this appropriation an Agricultural College must be established in accordance with an act of Congress approved July 2, 1862. The Legislative Assembly must assent to the purpose of said grant and provide to whom the payments of above mentioned appropriations shall be made. I earnestly urge that action looking to this very desirable end may be speedily taken. These suggestions tend naturally to a consideration of some method looking to the protection of the several grants from the government for educational and other purposes.

Many of our lands donated to the State for the support of common schools, being sections sixteen and thirty-six in every township, as well as university lands already selected, are endangered by trespassers and individuals asserting claims under the mineral land laws. Many of these lands are very valuable on account of their proximity to cities and towns; and this is doubtless the incentive in a majority of cases for jumping the same.

The result is that contests are now pending in the local land offices and the general land office at Washington involving our rights to school lands. Other cases of flagrant trespass in which lands are being occupied and despoiled have come to my knowledge but have not reached the land office or the courts. We have been virtually powerless in the absence of legislation to protect these sacred interests. It seems little less than a crime to see this splendid heritage passing away from us and falling into the hands of sordid and selfish individuals who take no account of the rights of the State. I think that a fund should be placed at the disposal of the Board of Land Commissioners for the payment of all necessary expenses of examination, survey and of contested cases involving the title or right of possession of school or other lands granted to the State. There should also be a State agent who should be empowered to represent our interests here and before the department at Washington. I commit the whole subject to your wisdom, profoundly conscious of the fact that no graver question will engage your attention.

RAILROAD GRANTS AND MINERAL LANDS.

The State has a direct interest in the speedy and final settlement of all questions affecting the grant of the Northern Pacific Railroad Company within our limits. First, we are vitally interested in upholding the spirit and purpose of the grant, which reserved all mineral land from its operation. These lands should always be open to exploration and development by the prospector and miner. The policy of the federal government has always run in that direction in an unbroken line, as evidenced by every public grant.

Second, it is of paramount importance to us to secure an early survey of such lands as the railroad company is entitled to under the law in order that this immense grant may be subjected to taxation like other property within the State.

It cannot be taxed before it is surveyed. The longer this indispensable condition is delayed, greater will be our misfortune in a financial point of view and greater will be the complications arising out of it.

It requires only a casual glance at the situation to see that for every legal subdivision claimed by the company which by decision of a competent tribunal shall be declared to be mineral, another section will be claimed in lieu thereof. Titles will be slandered, confusion generally will exist, and expensive litigation will follow.

It seems proper, therefore, that Congress should be memorialized to take such steps as it may seem to you just and expedient to designate and protect the mineral lands falling within the limits of the grant, and speedily to survey and designate all lands to which the railroad company is entitled, so that the same may be made to respond to their just proportion of the public burdens. In this connection I consider it proper to recommend for your investigation the question of the liability of the right of way of the Northern Pacific Railroad Company within this State to taxation.

Several propositions are involved. First, whether the clause of their charter exempting the right of way "within the Territories" is not destroyed by the creation of a State out of such Territory.

Second, does not the act admitting us as a State "upon an equal footing with the original States" operate *protanto* as a modification of the exemption clause of the charter? No such embargo was laid upon "the original States."

Third, does the provision of the charter providing for "modification," etc., contemplate such a modification as this?

Fourth, if it does and the creation of the State "upon an equal footing with the original States" is not tantamount to such a modification, would it not be well to direct the attention of our Senators and Representatives in Congress to the necessity of legislation to that end? It has come to my knowledge that the railroad companies maintain that this exemption is still in force.

DESERT LANDS AND IRRIGATION.

Every person who is conversant with our climate and the character of our soil must know that great possibilities await a general and comprehensive system of irrigation of our lands. I do not think the public is interested in holding a vast empire as a mere cattle range for large herds of stock. Upon the contrary it will be a glad day for Montana when the stock interests of the State shall be divided among the ranchmen in small lots. This will insure their proper feeding and shelter, and furnish employment to a large number of persons who must also be provided with the necessaries of life, all of which will be conducive of a more general prosperity to the State.

The proper solution of this question is pregnant with great import to the people of this State. There was a time when it seemed not improbable that the general government would take hold of this proposition and under its control and supervision manage the water supply to the advantage of all. It is perfectly apparent, however, at this time that influences are co-operating which will eventually destroy whatever hope we may have had in that direction. Eastern communities which set this opposition in motion, appear to be mindful only of local interests, and not of the prosperity of the whole country. Their protest is based upon the claim that the reclamation of these arid lands would subject the settler in the Eastern and Middle States to undue competition, retarding relief from agricultural depression. They will not, but they should remember that "this depression, arising from the competition of more favored conditions, is a portion of our inheritance and of the inalienable sacrifice exacted from mankind by that modern Juggernaut, Progress, whose wheels take no backward turn, however loud, however real, or however pitiful the outcries of the victims may be."

The homes which we propose to make are not for us alone, but for every citizen of the United States who has the courage to come and take one. We are interested in having this country settled and contribute something more to humanity and the world. There is no citizenship like that which is bound to the State and the Nation by a title in fee to the soil. Of course these lands, when reclaimed, will come in competition with that immense land grant of over twenty millions of acres almost wholly undisposed of in our State and possibly depreciate its value, but that is only another reason for their speedy reclamation, as it will secure cheap homes for the people and in the end benefit all. If we are to recieve any substantial or speedy benefits from our arid lands, I believe the State must first acquire a title to them and then undertake by appropriate legislation to reclaim and dispose of them. The Government should select, survey and convey these lands to the State upon such conditions as would secure their occupation and reclamation.

The West has contributed largely to building up the great revenues of the Nation and has received very slight corresponding benefits. It is not, however, the section, but the subject to be fostered and encouraged.

Agriculture lies at the foundation of our national prosperity. It is already languishing under the fatal pressure of unjust discrimination. It should be stimulated and promoted; not, however, by circumscribing its area, or diminishing the amount of its production, but the remedy lies in opening and extending by appropriate legislation our commercial relations with those countries which afford the most profitable markets for our products.

I think our demands on this subject should be formulated and transmitted to Congress.

INDIANS AND INDIAN RESERVATIONS.

The large Indian reservations within our borders which were set aside by the general government, embrace some of our best agricultural lands and are far in excess of the requirements of the Indians, who are no longer able or compelled to live by the chase, but in every instance are the recipients of bounty from the government. The buffalo and wild game which once abounded upon these great reservations are practically extinct, and with their departure disappeared the only reason for the maintenance of large areas of land for the occupancy of the Indians.

I therefore hope that you will memorialize Congress to compel a speedy selection and acceptance of these lands by individual members of Indian tribes, the destruction of tribal relations, and for an early restoration of the lands to the public domain.

Although there has been visible unrest among several tribes within the State, happily no serious outbreak has occurred within the last year. The only threatened danger grew out of the killing of a citizen and the indiscriminate slaughter of range cattle by the Cheyenne Indians in Eastern Montana last spring. The circumstances in this instance seemed to be of such importance as to justify sending a special messenger to the scene of the difficulty with instructions to investigate and report concerning the causes and probable consequences of the affair. Colonel C. D. Curtis. aide de camp, N. G. M., was accordingly detailed for the purpose and after conferring with the officers of the United States Army at Fort Keogh, proceeded to take the testimony of reliable and trustworthy citizens respecting the same, which was embodied in his report to the Executive office and which will be hereafter transmitted. An authentic copy of this report was forwarded to the Interior Department at Washington with the accompanying letter which probably, through the carelessness of some subordinate, was never acknowledged.

STATE OF MONTANA, EXECUTIVE OFFICE,
HELENA, MONTANA, July 3, 1890.

To the Secretary of the Interior, Washington, D. C.:

SIR: I have the honor to call your attention to the recent depredations of the Cheyenne Indians in Eastern Montana which resulted in the death of one citizen and the slaughter of numerous cattle upon the range. The citizens in Eastern Montana have been exposed to these depredations since the removal of the Cheyennes to Montana. Soon after the killing of Mr Ferguson I dispatched Colonel C. D. Curtis, aide de camp, N. G. M., to the scene of the trouble with instructions to investigate the cause of the same. A copy of his report is enclosed herewith.

I endorse the same as a report of a careful, competent and conscientious officer, who had ample facilities to ascertain the facts. I do not hesitate to say that the primary cause of the unrest and threatening attitude of these Indians is the result of a failure of the government to properly feed them. These Indians can not subsist on the meagre allowance doled out to them by the government. Such a course is a constant temptation to plunder, and then if unhappily detected, to kill the witness and thus remove the evidence against them.

I have the honor to submit, first, that these Indians do not, in fairness, belong to Montana, and ought to be removed.

Second, that if permitted to remain here they should be properly fed and kept upon the reservation and disarmed.

I very much fear that a recurrence of such trouble as detailed in Colonel Curtis' report, to which I ask your attention, will make it impossible to restrain the settlers in that remote section of the State from taking matters into their own hands.

I have the honor to be your obedient servant,

JOS. K. TOOLE,
Governor.

The conclusions reached in this letter are as true to-day as they were then. The continued disregard of our urgent but respectful protest manifests such a lamentable lack of interest in our protection that I trust you may find it expedient to give public expression to our affront by a proper memorial to Congress.

SALE, RENTAL AND DISTRIBUTION OF WATER.

One of the most salutary provisions in our declaration of rights is that which makes all the water now appropriated or which may hereafter be appropriated for sale, rental, distribution or other beneficial purposes, a public use. Under this provision I assume that you are invested with ample authority to provide by appropriate legislation, against excessive and extortionate charges by individuals, companies or corporations engaged in the sale, rental or distribution of water, and to prevent the unjust discrimination in the distribution of the same to the public. In my opinion, the right of the State to regulate this subject should be asserted and maintained. I accordingly invite your attention to this matter as one worthy of your early consideration.

HOMESTEAD AND EXEMPTION.

Homestead and exemption laws are the outgrowth of our civilization, and in all enlightened communities there is a universal concurrence of sentiment in favor of making them broad and liberal. Society owes something to the wife and children and the creditor who trusts the reckless and improvident, ought not to be permitted to pursue the former to destitution. I therefore recommend that in obedience to the Constitution, liberal homestead and exemption laws be enacted.

PRINTING.

Provision should be made for carrying out section 30, article 5, of the Constitution respecting public printing.

Sec. 30. All stationery, printing, paper, fuel and light used in the legislative and other departments of government shall be furnished and the printing and binding and distribution of the laws, journals, and department reports and other printing and binding, and the repairing and furnishing the halls and rooms used for the meeting of the Legislative Assembly and its committees shall be performed under contract, to be given to the lowest responsible bidder, below such maximum price and under such regulations as may be prescribed by law. No member or officer of any department of the government shall be in any way interested in any such contract; and all such contracts shall be subject to the approval of the governor and the State treasurer.

The present contract with the Journal Publishing Company, entered into under the Territorial law, and which was continued in force by the Constitution, expires on the 11th day of March, 1891.

THE SUPREME COURT.

Under the provisions of section 3, article 8, of the Constitution, the Supreme Court is empowered to summon a jury when required to determine an issue of fact. It will be necessary for the Legislature to prescribe by law the manner in which such jury shall be summoned. There is no statute which governs this contingency.

Under the provisions of section 4, of the same article, the Legislative Assembly should fix the time for holding the terms of the Supreme Court, or confer the authority upon the justices to regulate them. I think the number of terms should be increased to four, and that the Legislative Assembly should designate them. This legislation would secure a speedy hearing of the appeals and render certain the day when they could be heard.

CLERK OF THE SUPREME COURT.

The Constitution has deemed the office of the Clerk of the Supreme Court of such importance that it has required him to be elected by the people of the State. The fee allowed for his services should be revised, and when collected should be paid into the treasury. This officer should receive a salary.

DISTRICT COURTS.

Since our admission into the Union we have been working under an entirely new judicial system. In the main it has proven satisfactory, and with some slight modifications and legislation which was designed in the first instance to give it effect, I am confident that it will meet every requirement demanded by the public.

Hon. W. W. Dixon, the Chairman of the Judiciary Committee of the late Constitutional Convention, has so succinctly reviewed the system in a recent address before the Society of the Framers of the Constitution that I submit an extract therefrom. Among other things he said:

"In the Counties of Lewis and Clarke and Silver Bow the old courts were so much behind in the trial of causes when the present judges took their seats, and business has since so increased that the new courts have been unable to afford litigants in civil cases the prompt trials which they should have.

"The judges have worked very industriously, but can make little progress. In each of these Counties an additional judge is needed, at least for one or two years to come, and the Legislative Assembly should so provide.

"In those districts where several Counties are united the system seems generally to work satisfactorily. Some of these Counties, however, have so increased in population and business that they desire and are entitled to be made separate districts, and this, I think, should be done as speedily as may be. It is to be hoped that in a few years each County in the State will be a district with its own judge. When this is done, all the benefits of the judicial system established by the Constitution will be realized.

"One trouble and inconvenience I have heard mentioned in the Counties joined with others in one district, is the delay in procuring orders in probate matters when the Judge is absent from the County where the order is desired. This, I think, might be remedied to a considerable extent by an amendment to the probate practice act, authorizing the Clerk of the Court to make, in the absence of the Judge, such orders as are usually made exparte.

"Section 8, article 3, of the Constitution, provides for the prosecution of criminal offenses in the District Court by information, and also by indictment by a grand jury, when the Court considers it necessary to summon one, and a grand jury is to consist of seven persons, only, of whom five must concur to find an indictment.

"Owing to the unfortunate political complications of last winter, which deprived us of much needed legislation to make Constitutional provisions effective, we have no law defining or providing for information. The Supreme Court has therefore held, and no doubt correctly, that criminal cases must still be prosecuted by indictment. We have not therefore enjoyed the benefits of the provision which dispenses in most cases with a grand jury, but we have reduced the number comprising it to seven. This has reduced the expense of the Counties and I think has been found satisfactory to the people. The Constitutional provision that in case of misdemeanor, and in all civil actions, two-thirds in number of the jury may render a verdict has, so far as I have seen or been informed, been found to be very satisfactory in practical operation and has greatly facilitated the decision of cases and prevented expense and unnecessary new trials."

By promptly providing for proceedings by information, heavy bills of cost will be saved which now necessarily obtain. If witnesses are compelled to attend at preliminary examinations, before the grand jury and then upon the trial, three separate bills of cost are incurred when one ought to answer the purpose; besides, the witnesses are frequently of a migratory character, can not be found, or if so, at heavy expense on account of mileage.

The necessity of another judge in Lewis and Clark and Silver Bow Counties is apparent to every one who has considered the subject. A letter addressed to this office from Hon. W. H. Hunt, Judge of the First Judicial Court, giving a statement of the volume of business transacted in his district and the immediate demand for relief, is clear, concise and convincing. The same is appended hereto and marked "Exhibit D." I may add that the reasons given by Judge Hunt are equally applicable to Silver Bow County, and that the same would have been made manifest by the judge of that district but for his unavoidable absence at this time.

CODE COMMISSION.

The important work of preparing the four codes authorized by the act of March 14, 1889, was committed to a commission which was required to report three of the codes to the next ensuing Legislature. The commission has been industriously engaged in the work since the adoption of the State Constitution, and has completed and filed with the Secretary of State the "Civil Code," the "Code of Civil Proceedure" and "Penal Code." I am in receipt of a com-

EXECUTIVE OFFICE. 39

munication from the Chairman of the Commission under date of December 11, 1890, as follows:

"Replying to yours of the 10th I have the honor to report: That the Code Commission appointed in pursuance of the act of the Legislative Assembly of March 11, 1889, commenced its labors in April, 1889, and almost continuously since the first day of September of that year, has worked in codifying the laws as provided in the act, and as a result the Code Commission has completed and filed with the Secretary of State a "Civil Code," a "Code of Civil Procedure," a "Penal Code," and is now at work upon a "Political Code," which, it is expected, will be completed by the 15th day of January, 1891.

"The making of the Political Code is a great task and ought to have been completed before the making of the other codes, but this could not be done and comply with the act creating the Commission. Much labor has been spent upon the Political Code in making our laws, offices, official duties, and State and County governments generally conform to the requirements of the Constitution. The Commission might profitably have spent every day since the passage of the act creating it, upon the Political Code.

"We have felt hurried with our work on account of the limited time given for its completion. In other States, from three to five years have been occupied by commissioners in codifying each subdivision of their laws, and we would be much better satisfied with our work if we had more time to bestow upon it.

"Before the codes, already filed, are finally submitted, a few changes will have to be made in consequence of some of the provisions of the Political Code, but we hope to have all the codes ready by the 15th day of January next.

"To make each code complete and harmonious with itself, and with each of the other codes, and at the same time embody and perfect the provisions of our Territorial statutes and make them conform to the Constitution, has required a vast amount of patience and labor, and two years further time might well be spent in the work."

These codes will embrace the whole body of the statute law of the State, except such additions as may be made at this session. The greatest possible care and investigation will of course be necessary in order to preserve harmony between their several parts, and consistency between the whole and the Constitution. While the gentlemen composing the Commission are learned in the law, and are in every way qualified for such distinguished and important service, nothing effecting the character of their work should be taken by implication on that account. The responsibility for the work will rest jointly upon us and the Commission. The act creating the Commission contemplated that five hundred copies of the several codes should be printed and placed in the hands of the State Librarian, judges of the Supreme and District Courts and other State officers, and members of the bar of the State, in order that the work might be intelligently examined and criticised before the assembling of the Legislature. There does not seem to have been any appropriation available for this purpose, at all events none were published. It will not be unwise to consider in the outset whether it will not be more prudent to first provide for the printing contemplated by the act creating the Commission and then confine your labors to the enactment of such legislation as is necessary to carry out Constitutional provisions and the settlement of outstanding claims against this State, leaving the code to be considered by the next Legislature. Indeed, this may be necessary, as the Constitution requires that every bill shall be printed before its passage.

This is an important question and worthy of your consideration.

PUBLIC SCHOOLS.

There is abundant evidence to show that our public school system has improved steadily from year to year. It is the great popular institution of the State and deserves well of the Legislative Assembly. Reliable statistics show the following interesting facts: There are about thirty thousand school children in the State. About six hundred teachers are employed at an average of about fifty-six dollars per month. One million dollars is invested in school property. This includes three hundred and forty-nine school houses, but excludes private schools. At the close of the school year, August 31, 1889, the several Counties had on hand $64,761.78. Total amount received for school purposes from taxation and other sources for 1889, $569,521.91.

```
Paid teachers.................................$215,578 02
Paid for school apparatus......................   6,807 16
Paid for library...............................     276 87
Paid for school houses, sites, etc.............  88,613 50
Paid other expenses............................  32,079 57
Balance on hand August 31, 1890................ 244,119 97
```

During the year forty-seven school districts observed Arbor Day and 250 trees were planted. The compulsory clause of the school law has not been generally observed, but no prosecutions have been instituted under it.

FEES OF COUNTY OFFICERS.

Your attention is directed to the present fee bill of the respective County officers. The complaint is universal that the fees under the Territorial laws, and which are now injected into the State statutes, are unreasonable and excessive. While all officers should have a fair and just compensation, and ought to be consulted in the establishment of fees, the citizen ought not to be compelled to surrender entirely to their demands. I recommend, therefore, a complete revision and adjustment of the present law fixing the fees of County officers so as to make them approximately commensurate with the services rendered, and that all fees when collected be paid into the respective County treasuries, and that in lieu thereof, salaries be paid to such officers.

I feel confident that this will withdraw the temptation to be over zealous, ostensibly for the public good, but in reality not infrequently for their own aggrandizement. At all events it is worth the experiment, but in my judgment it should not take effect until January, A. D. 1893.

CORPORATIONS.

The organization of corporations to carry on large enterprises has become a necessity in this and other States. The development of our resources and the carrying forward of projects for the public good in many instances are of such magnitude, and require the outlay of such large sums of money, that private capital can not be enduced to embark in them. The law should provide for the incorporation of such, but I condem as bad legislation the existing statute, inherited from the Territory, which permits almost every character of business and industry to become the subject of an incorporation, whereby the liability of the stockholder is limited. No one but a creditor is entitled to see the books of the corporation, and hence a person dealing with such concern in the first instance, is at a disadvantage. I recommend the modification of existing laws so that corporations may be formed for the following and such other purposes as may be considered proper, and which shall be specifically provided for, and no other:

1. The support of public worship.
2. The support of any benevolent, charitable, educational or missionary undertaking.
3. The support of any literary or scientific undertaking, the maintenance of a library or the promotion of painting, music or other fine arts.
4. The encouragement of agriculture or horticulture.
5. The maintenance of a club for social enjoyment.
6. The maintenance of public parks, and the facilities for skating and other innocent sports.
7. The maintenance of a public or private cemetery.
8. The prevention and punishment of theft or wilful injury to property and insurance against such risks.
9. The insurance of human life and dealing in annuities.
10. The insurance of human beings against sickness or personal injuries.
11. The insurance of lives of domestic animals.
12. The insurance of property against marine risks.
13. The insurance of property against loss or injury by fire or by any risk of inland transportation.
14. Transaction of a banking business.
15. The construction and maintenance of a railway and of a telegraph line in connection therewith.
16. The construction and maintenance of any other species of roads, and bridges in connection therewith.
17. The construction and maintenance of a bridge.
18. The construction and maintenance of a telegraph line.
19. The establishment and maintenance of a stage line.
20. The establishment and maintenance of a ferry.

21. The building and navigation of steamboats, and carriage of persons and property thereon.

22. The supply of water to the public.

23. The manufacture and supply of gas, or the supply of any motive power, light or heat to the public.

24. The transaction of any manufacturing, mining, mechanical or chemical business.

25. The transaction of a printing or publishing business.

26. The establishment and maintenance of a hotel.

27. The erection of buildings and accumulation and loan of funds for the purchase of real property.

28. The improvement of the breed of domestic animals by importation, sale or otherwise, or

29. The construction of canals and reservoirs for conveying and storing water and the boring of artesian wells.

REGISTRATION.

The Constitution gives the Legislature power to enact suitable registration laws. The schedule annexed to the Constitution provides for continuing in force all laws of the Territory not inconsistent with the Constitution, or the Constitution and laws of the United States. By this, the registration law enacted by the last Territorial Legislature becomes a part of our State statutes. While the Legislature ought to throw around the ballot every safeguard against fraud and repeating, and a proper registration law is conducive to that end, the present system overshoots the mark and operates to disfranchise many good citizens or this State whose votes are entitled to be cast and counted. In my opinion no registration should be required as a condition precedent to voting, in remote and sparsely settled communities. The facilities for transportation are inadequate in such sections of the country, and those afforded are expensive and often beyond the means of the voters. Mountain ranges are sometimes required to be crossed and the distance required to be traveled has been shown to be, in some instances, as much as a hundred miles, and not unfrequently from twelve to twenty miles. The result of this is that the ranchman, the stock-herder and the prospector, who form a large per cent. of our population, and who are generally impecunious and unable to bear the burden of such an expense and the loss of time, as the present system necessarily entails, are compeled to remain at home and are thereby disfranchised on election day. To obviate this wrong done to the citizen, I recommend that the present registration law be so amended that registration shall not be required except in incorporated cities and towns having a given population. It is in the latter places, the centers of population, where law-breakers and malefactors congregate that repeating and fraud are practiced, and not in remote precincts where every man knows his neighbor and a stranger is at once observed. I believe that it is an undue and unnecessary burden on the citizen to require him to register every time there is a general election. Having once registered that ought to be sufficient for at least six years.

Provision should be made whereby the elector who has once registered and removed will not lose the right of sufferage.

Aside from this the law is unreasonable and probably would be declared void upon a proceeding involving its consideration in the courts. First, because it undertakes to disfranchise a large number of voters through no fault of their own, to-wit: Those who are ill and unable to attend before registration officers, but who are able to attend upon election day. Second, because it makes an unjust and unlawful distinction between the rights of native born and naturalized citizens and electors, to-wit: It requires a naturalized voter to produce his certificate of naturalization or show by evidence other than his own oath that such certificate was issued, while it permits a native born citizen to prove his standing as a voter by his own oath. Third, it destroys the right of suffrage of those citizens whose qualifications as respects residence would mature between the 15th day of October and election day, the registration board having adjourned on October 15. The Constitution authorizes the Legislature to enact "registration and such other laws as may be necessary to secure the purity of elections and guard against abuses of the elective franchise," but this does not authorize by direction or by indirection the disfranchisement, without his own fault or negligence, any elector under the Constitution.

Section 2, article 10, of the Constitution, makes the term of residence apply to a time immediately "preceeding the election," so that in order to give the citizens the right of suffrage guaranteed by the Constitution he should be permitted to register on the day preceeding the election. These questions were considered at length in the case of the Attorney General vs. the City of Detroit, and decided by the Supreme Court of Michigan on December 28, 1889, and reported in Vol. 41, No. 13, of the Albany Law Journal, from which I make the following extract:

"Why should a person claiming to be an elector by naturalization be debarred, if he has lost his certificate, from establishing such fact by his own oath? A person may swear that he is native born, and he is not required also to prove this fact by some one else, before he can be registered; but if he wishes to show that he is an elector by naturalization, he is presumed to be unable himself to tell the truth under oath, and must be corroborated by some one else. The easiest way for a person of this class, wishing to cast a fraudulent vote, would simply be to swear that he was born in the United States, and in such a case a perjurer is put to less trouble to get on the registry list than an honest man who desires to show that he has been naturalized, but who, unfortunately has lost the record evidence of such naturalization. This distinction between native born and naturalized electors is an unfair one, and, as above shown, entirely unnecessary in order to prevent fraud. Its tendency will be to disfranchise honest men and to induce dishonest men to perjure themselves. Section 13, in reference to removals from one precinct to another and the necessary steps to become registered in such cases, seems to me most unreasonable and unnecessary; but perhaps this is within the power of the

Legislature, as it is not absolutely impossible to comply with it. But in relation to naturalized voters, the very men who have probably lost their certificates, and can not now replace them, are elderly men, who have been naturalized for many years, and have exercised the elective franchise in Detroit without question for upward of a quarter of a century. They have, many of them, no doubt forgotten the particular name of the court in which they took out their papers; and to prove their issue by some one other than themselves would be, in some instances, impossible. A law that treats these men as men whose oaths can not be taken in their own interest, while it permits a native born citizen to prove his standing as a voter by his own testimony can not receive my sanction, as I believe such a requirement to be not only unjust and unfair, but unconstitutional, unless applied to all. Another distinction may also be noted. A native born citizen becoming of age between the last day of registration and the election, is permitted to vote; but a foreign born citizen, who has taken out his first papers, and whose right to full citizenship or the elective franchise, will ripen between the completion of the registry list and the opening of the polls, can not vote.

"In my opinion, no registry law is valid which deprives an elector of his Constitutional right to vote by any regulation with which it is impossible for him to comply. No elector can lose his right to vote, the highest exercise of a freeman's will except by his own fault or negligence. If the legislature, under the pretext of regulation, can destroy this Constitutional right by annexing an additional qualification as to the number of days such voter must reside within a precinct before he can vote therein or any other requisite, in direct opposition to any of the Constitutional requirements, then it can as well require of the elector entirely new qualifications, independent of the Constitution, before the right of suffrage can be exercised. If the exigencies of the times are such, which I do not believe, that a fair and honest election can not be held in the City of Detroit, or in any other place in our State, without other qualifications and restrictions upon both native born and naturalized citizens than those found in and authorized by the Constitution, then the remedy is with the people to alter such Constitution by the lawful methods pointed out by that instrument."

I therefore recommend such modifications of existing laws as will remedy the evils pointed out.

PURITY OF THE BALLOT.

The last Territorial Legislature inaugurated a ballot reform that is worthy of note. While the Australian system of voting, as a whole, does not come up to public expectation, it is, nevertheless, a departure in the right direction, and its general acceptance by the people, with some modifications, is in my opinion assured. There should be no abatement of public interest in legislation designed to secure and perpetuate the purity of the ballot. The present law would be just as effective as it was designed to be it, instead of printing the names of all the candidates on one continuous ticket, their names should be on separate tickets representing the party whose political principles they avowed, or upon the same ticket in separate columns, I recommend this modification of the law. The present system is tantamount to an educational qualificacation on the one hand, or a complete surrender upon the other to judges of election, who, in many cases are incompetent and in some cases venal. The time is too short to point out the many imperfections of a law which was well intended, but which to the most casual observer, in the light of observation and actual experience, has been demonstrated to be very crude. If this system can be simplified and at the same time preserve its essential qualities, in my opinion, it will popularize politics and in the end secure the most perfect reflection of the popular will of any system ever inaugurated. It stimulates courage in the dependent to vote according to his conscientious convictions, and above all, it strikes savagely at the method of machine politics and promises its complete annihilation. In other words, simplified and properly guarded, it secures to the voter the largest freedom of thought. independence of action and exercise of judgment of any system which has ever obtained to my knowledge. So certain am I of the salutary effect of this system that I venture to predict it will never be abandoned until the State is ready to abandon its sovereignty.

If our institutions are to endure, and the honor, integrity and prosperity of the State are to continue to be the hope and anchor of the citizen, the vote of the people expressed at the polls without hinderance or intimidation must be sedulously guarded and maintained at all hazards. The duties of the officers charged with the responsibility of declaring the result of an election should be made so explicit and the punishment for misconduct so severe that the temptation for venal treachery at vital points will be forever removed. I call your attention to the unusual and unnecessary expense in the matter of printing which the present election law entails upon the people. It should be framed to meet only necessary and proper expenses.

PRESIDENTIAL ELECTORS.

Before another Legislature shall have assembled an election for President and Vice-President of the United States will occur. Provision should therefore be made as contemplated by the United States statutes upon this subject and for canvassing the votes, declaring the result and so forth.

NOTARIES PUBLIC.

Under the law there is no limitation to the number of Notaries permitted to be appointed. The convenience which such an officer has been found to be, especially in remote and sparsely settled communities, has led me to appoint such in every case where the applicant possessed the necessary qualifications. There have been 369 Notaries appointed and commissioned since the 8th day of November, A. D. 1889. Not a single case of malfeasance or misconduct in office has come under my observation or been brought to my attention.

REWARDS.

Under Territorial law the Governor was authorized to offer rewards for the apprehension of persons charged or convicted of crimes, in his discretion, in amount not exceeding one thousand dollars. No rewards have been offered during my term of office.

Two rewards, aggregating one thousand dollars, were offered by Governor White, late Governor of the Territory, for the apprehension of two Indians, charged with murder. The Indians were apprehended, as claimed by the Sheriff of Missoula county, the county in which the crimes were committed. They have since been convicted, and the Sheriff of that county claims the reward.

Public policy, however, it seems, is opposed to paying a reward to an officer for doing an act, which by law, it is his duty to perform; and I have been constrained to withhold the approval of this account. I also call your attention to the fact that the existing law seems to appropriate money for a reward in arresting a prisoner, but no appropriation is expressly made for the payment of a reward for the apprehension of a person not a "prisoner." In other words, an escape seems to be necessary before the appropriation is available.

PROTECTION OF RANGES AND TIMBER FROM FIRE.

Section 3, article 19, of the Constitution is as follows:

Sec. 3. The Legislative Assembly will enact suitable laws to prevent the destruction by fire from any cause of the grasses and forests upon lands of the State or upon lands of the public domain, the control of which may be conferred by Congress upon this State and to otherwise protect the same.

In this State, where so much is made to depend upon the preservation of the ranges, every possible protection and safeguard consistent with property rights, and a full enjoyment of the same, should be invoked to prevent prairie fires, there ought to be a community of interest in this behalf. I am of the opinion that nothing could be done more conducive to this than the passage of a law by which railroad companies operating in the State should be compelled to burn their right of way annually, and thus prevent a spread of fire originating not infrequently from sparks from their engines and the cleaning of fire boxes.

LOTTERY AND GIFT ENTERPRISES.

Section 2, article 19, of the Constitution is as follows:

"Sec. 2. The Legislative Assembly shall have no power to authorize lotteries or gift enterprises for any purpose, and shall pass laws to prohibit the sale of lottery or gift enterprise tickets in the State."

This legislation should be enacted and penalties prescribed. A question has arisen whether existing laws apply to the sale of lottery tickets in any lottery drawing to take place outside of the State. It should be made specific. The Supreme Court of the United States, speaking of the demoralizing effect of such concerns, says:

"Experience has shown that the common forms of gambling are comparatively inocuous when placed in contrast with the wide-spread pestilence of lotteries. The former are confined to a few persons and places, but the latter infests the whole community. It enters every dwelling; it reaches every class; it preys upon the earnings of the poor; it plunders the ignorant and the simple."

Our legislation on the subject should be so comprehensive and the penalties so severe as to close forever every avenue of approach to this insidious and demoralizing foe of society.

TO PROMOTE UNIFORMITY OF LAWS.

A commendable effort is being put forth by the American Bar Association, seconded by a number of the States, to secure uniformity of legislation throughout the United States, especially with regard to marriage and divorce, wills, descent and distribution of property, form of deeds, acknowledgments and kindred topics.

There are but two modes of securing this end. First, an amendment to the Federal Constitution. Second, uniform action by the States. The first method was not feasible or practicable. Your attention is invited to the second method, voluntary action by the several States. The Legislature of the State of New York has taken the initiative in this matter and has passed the following law:

Sec. 1. Within thirty days after the passage of this Act, the Governor shall appoint by, and with the consent of the Senate, three Commissioners, who are by her Constitution a Board of Commissioners by the name and style of "commissioners for the promotion of uniformity of legislation in the United States." It shall be the duty of said Board to examine the subject of marriage and divorce, insolvency, the form of notarial certificates and other subjects; to ascertain the best means of effect and assimilation and uniformity in the laws of the States, and especially to consider whether it would be wise and practicable for the State of New York to invite the other States of the Union to send representatives to a convention to draft uniform laws to be submitted for the approval and adoption of the several States and to devise and recommend such other course of action as shall best accomplish the purpose of this Act."

Such anomolies as sometimes arise under the laws of the different States respecting the subjects referred to, ought not to exist. It is recommended, therefore, that action be taken looking to our co-operation in some plan to promote this very desirable end.

EXPENSE OF CONSTITUTIONAL CONVENTION.

The $20,000 appropriated by Congress to defray the expenses of holding the late Constitutional Convention was found to be inadequate for that purpose. Additional clerk hire and other officers, including a stenographer, and a stenographic report of the proceedings of the convention, was by resolution of the convention declared to be necessary and proper for the convenience and early dispatch of business. To cover these extra expenses the convention adopted an ordinance appropriating the following sums for the following purposes respectively, and declared the same to be charges against the State of Montana. The item for the stenographic report is an approximation but of course is capable of being rendered certain when the report is filed.

John Trumbull, clerk	$ 220 00
E. C. Garrett, clerk	215 00
John McKay, clerk	220 00
Lee Swords, clerk	215 00
Edward Kerr, clerk	215 00
Henry Bernard, clerk	215 00
Miss Jennie Merriman, clerk	160 00
William Taylor, clerk	55 00
William Green, asst. sergt. at arms	175 00
Morris Langhorne, page	172 00
Cornelius Hedges, page	172 00
Wm. D. Alexander, page	172 00
Henry Bernard, for supervising the printing of the constitution and typewriting	100 00
Lee Swords, for acting as clerk to the committee on address	25 00
C. P. Connolly, stenographer	675 00
C. P. Connolly, transcript of proceedings and debates of Constitutional Convention (estimated)	1,800 00
Printing 20,000 copies of the constitution (estimated)	2,100 00
Total	$6,906 00

I, therefore, recommend that the same be paid by the State and that Congress be memorialized to reimburse the State as it intended by its enabling act to cover all expenses of the convention. Inasmuch as this ordinance was not submitted to the people for ratification and by them ratified, legislation is required to give it effect. Similar deficiencies growing out of the admission of North and South Dakota and Washington were allowed by the last Congress, but owing to some imperfection of our proofs or otherwise Montana's claim was omitted.

CONSTITUTIONAL AMENDMENTS.

Conscious of the fact that the Constitutional Convention, which formulated and adopted our Constitution, committed a grievous mistake in providing for the apportionment and representation of Senators by which population, the only just basis of representation under our form of government was wholly ignored, I call upon the Legislative Assembly at the first opportunity to provide for the early submission of a constitutional amendment whereby this inequality may be speedily corrected.

THE WORLD'S COLUMBIAN EXPOSITION.

The propriety of taking such steps as may be necessary to enable Montana to be creditably represented at the World's Columbian Exposition to be held in Chicago in 1893, by virtue of an Act of Congress approved April 25,

1860, will be for your determination. I have every reason to believe that this exposition will be the crowning glory of the nineteenth century, and that no better opportunity will be offered of placing before the world in an attractive form the great and varied resources and illimitable possibilities of our young State than that furnished at this great exposition.

I would be glad to let the world know with what prodigality nature has endowed us and call attention to the splendid field which our State offers for intelligent exploration and development. Every phase of our wealth-producing resources should be made manifest and fully exemplified, including a practical application of the principles of irrigation so simple and yet so little understood and appreciated.

Under the act creating the commission, A. H. Mitchell, of Deer Lodge county, and L. H. Hershfield, of Lewis and Clarke county were appointed by the president of the United States as commissioners to represent the State of Montana upon said commission. T. E. Collins, of Cascade county and Benjamin F. White, of Beaverhead county, were appointed their alternates.

Mrs. Lily Rosecrans Toole, of Lewis and Clark county, and Mrs. H. Knippenberg, of Beaverhead county were by the president of the commission, upon the recommendation of the commissioners of this State, appointed upon the board of lady managers. Mrs. Mariam D. Cooper, of Gallatain county and Mrs. F. I. Worden, of Missoula county, their alternates. Montana was complimented by the appointment of Mrs. Mary Harrison, of Montana, as a lady manager at large; and also the only vice-president at large; thus making our State one of the eight with a representation of three lady managers on the board.

ADMISSION DAY.

I recommend that the 8th day of November, the day of our admission into the Union, be declared a legal holiday.

GREAT SEAL OF THE STATE.

A State Seal should be adopted as well as seals for the several courts and commissions.

The time in which you are limited to do the work of the session is scarcely adequate, but much can be accomplished. Concerning the foregoing recommendations and all other proper subjects of legislation, you may rely upon my cordial co-operation.   JOS. K. TOOLE, Governor.

Executive Office, Helena, Mont., Jan. 5, A. D. 1891.

EXHIBIT A.

STATEMENT SHOWING ASSESSMENTS OF COUNTIES FOR 1889 AND 1890, WITH INCREASE OR DECREASE IN 1889 OVER 1890.

COUNTIES.	1889.	1890.	Increase.	Decrease.
Beaverhead	$ 3,128,078	$ 3,013,172	$	$ 114,906
Choteau	4,155,281	4,950,217	794,936	....
Custer	4,465,411	6,380,177	1,919,766	....
Cascade	4,311,690	8,648,548	4,334,858	....
Dawson	1,742,887	2,406,681	663,794	....
Deer Lodge	7,826,645	9,900,491	2,073,846	....
Fergus	2,985,851	3,299,475	313,624	....
Gallatin	4,320,570	4,643,119	322,549	....
Jefferson	3,167,714	3,919,400	751,686	....
Lewis and Clarke	15,437,096	26,708,717	11,271,621	....
Madison	2,752,651	3,035,456	281,805	....
Meagher	2,866,802	4,043,437	1,136,635	....
Missoula	4,982,716	8,113,188	3,130,472	....
Park	3,062,900	4,492,436	1,429,536	....
Silver Bow	11,368,572	16,208,833	4,840,261	....
Yellowstone	2,872,080	3,217,037	414,957	....
Totals	$ 79,376,944	$112,373,384	$ 33,675,346	$ 114,906

EXHIBIT B.

STATEMENT SHOWING NET INDEBTEDNESS OF THE SEVERAL COUNTIES MARCH 1, 1890, AND INCREASE AND DECREASE FOR THE YEAR ENDING FEBRUARY 28, 1890.

COUNTIES.	Indebtedness Mar. 1, 1889.	Indebtedness Mar. 1, 1890.	Increase.	Decrease.
Beaverhead	$ 37,869.22	$ 76,303.08	$ 38,433.86	$ ....
Choteau	124,562.27	124,294.05	....	268.22
Custer	245,733.83	260,979.50	15,245.97	....
Cascade	69,801.06	53,019.22	....	16,781.84
Dawson	132,671.47	125,181.96	....	7,489.51
Deer Lodge	106,947.31	139,676.15	32,728.84	....
Fergus	19,239.97	18,295.30	....	944.67
Gallatin	65,717.90	57,591.55	....	8,126.35
Jefferson	121,464.22	154,549.35	33,085.13	....
Lewis and Clarke	163,167.44	125,679.15	....	37,488.29
Madison	....	87,229.00	....	....
Meagher	55,318.26	81,076.13	25,757.87	....
Missoula	165,762.46	223,839.73	58,077.27	....
Park	55,674.68	64,379.18	8,704.50	....
Silver Bow	125,000.00	77,281.11	....	47,718.89
Yellowstone	120,392.87	125,649.18	4,256.31	....
Totals	$1,609,322.66	$1,794,023.64	$ 216,289.75	$ 118,817.77

EXHIBIT C.

STATEMENT SHOWING THE CONDITION OF THE SEVERAL FUNDS AND THE AMOUNT CONTRIBUTED TO EACH BY THE RESPECTIVE COUNTIES.

Counties.	General Fund.	Stock In-spection.	Stock In-demnity.	Sheep In-spection.	Auditor.	Secretary of State.	Boiler In-spection.	Escheats.	Totals.
Beaverhead	7,131 80	444 35		63 19					7,639 21
Choteau	17,633 63	592 83							18,312 74
Custer	9,697 35	1,925 79	625 44	86 28					11,750 26
Cascade	8,608 21	2,811 05	922 11	103 68					12,460 21
Dawson	1,985 57	187 34	62 31	48 84					2,207 58
Deer Lodge	33,749 89	753 49	232 08	72 06			60 88	35,357 36
Fergus	8,149 05	1,951 69	629 37				747 21	12,445 14
Gallatin	11,406 01		46 23	986 82				11,529 54
Jefferson	9,768 29	915 71	292 44	48 57				11,089 29
Lewis and Clarke	48,926 31	466 85	157 01	32 31		2,315 50	1,455 34	54,521 11
Madison	7,430 98	1,225 48	363 85	5 01				10,705 75
Meagher	8,391 51	1,128 15	198 82		2,580 40			10,516 54
Missoula	17,861 85		178 02	848 08			21,618 20	39,659 08
Park	11,291 67	7 56	64 28					11,450 51
Silver Bow	47,450 63	16 38	73 33	31			3,887 00	51,447 15
Yellowstone	6,181 80	928 61	38 62	272 31				7,441 31
Totals	255,564 30	12,361 48	4,189 40	2,253 52	2,580 40	2,315 50	3,887 00	24,460 63	308,595 23

EXHIBIT D.

AMOUNT OF CLAIMS AGAINST THE STATE. (APPROXIMATED.)

Sheriffs' claims for board in county jail..........................$	8,727	95
Claims account requisition papers.............................	652	70
Bounty certificates..	11,501	00
State prison contractors—		
Prisoners at 70 cents per day......................$19,250 00		
Prisoners at 65 cents per day...................... 20,595 90		
	39,845	90
National Guard claims—		
Annual appropriation (company)..................$ 6,750 00		
Other claims.................................... 7,012 50		
	13,762	50
State board of arbitration.......................................	290	40
Claims for printing..	6,515	80
Claims for care and maintenance of the insane—		
Amount for maintenance.......................$69,065 97		
Amount for clothing and cash................... 1,330 50		
	70,396	47
Claims account of Legislature,................................	2,325	30
Claims for transportation of deaf mutes from institutes to Montana,		
note given by State officers for amount—		
Amount of note...............................$ 700 00		
Interest.. 46 00		
	746	00
Claims on writs of habeas corpus..............................	208	90
Claims for making arrest by warrant from Lieutenant Governor,		
(no certificate issued for this claim)........................	195	00
Rewards...	1,000	00
	$156,168	42

EXHIBIT E.

HELENA, MONTANA, December 23, 1890.

To His *Excellency,*
    JOS. K. TOOLE.
        Governor of Montana.

DEAR SIR: I have the honor to herewith submit for your consideration a statement of the business transacted by the District Court of the first judicial district of the State, from the date of the admission of the State, November 8th, 1889, up to and including the 22d day of December, 1890. Court was regularly opened for business on November 9th, 1889, and has continually been in session since that date, except upon holidays and during the month of August when I was out of the State.

    I respectfully call your attention to the fact that there has been a steady increase in business for the last three years, and invite your attention to the volume of business which has been transacted during the past thirteen months as well as to the large number of cases still undisposed of, and which is increasing every day. During the time that I have occupied the bench I have done my utmost to dispose of the old cases which I found upon the calendar when the State was admitted. Many of these cases were important, and consumed much time in disposition.

The experience of the past thirteen months clearly demonstrates, I think, the need of another judge in this district. It is a very severe task upon one man to hold court each and every day, and give to the important questions that consideration that is due to the propositions of law presented and that a judge feels that he should and would like to give. I do not hesitate, therefore, to express to you my earnest hope that you may deem it fit to recommend to the Legislature the enactment of a law by which there may be two judges and two departments of our District Court.

I have conferred with nearly all the members of the bar and so far as I am able to judge their wish is unanimous for the relief suggested. As to the provisions of the law creating a new judgeship, it is unnecessary for me to make any suggestions, unless called upon to do so. I have the honor, sir, to remain your obedient servant. WILLIAM H. HUNT,
Judge First Judicial District.

STATEMENT.

Civil cases on docket when State was admitted.................... 501
New cases since November 8, 1889............................. 721

    Total number of civil cases................................ 1,222
Criminal cases commenced since November 8, 1889............... 142
Insane cases tried by juries, pursuant to law, from November 8, 1889 21
                                                           163

    Total number of cases, civil, criminal and insane.............. 1,385

CONTRA.

Civil cases disposed of and finally determined from November 8, 1889 580
Criminal cases disposed of from November 8, 1889................ 141
Insane cases disposed of from November 8, 1889.................. 21
    Total number of cases entirely disposed of since November 8, 1889 742
    Cases yet to be disposed of on the docket.................... 643
                                                          1,385

There have been also 71 new cases filed for probate from November 8, 1889.

Veto Message.

THE STATE OF MONTANA, } ss.
    EXECUTIVE OFFICE.

                    HELENA, MONTANA, March 4th, 1891.
To the Senate:
    I return herewith without my approval and with my objections Senate

bill No. 10. "An Act to amend sections 446, 460, 467, 468 and 472 of Chapter 25, Fifth Division, General Laws of Montana relating to Corporations for Industrial or Productive purposes."

The purpose of this bill appears to be to confer the benefits and privileges of the incorporation act upon mercantile establishments, and to extend the time of incorporations to fifty years.

The custom of forming private corporations for the purpose of engaging in undertakings which are proper subjects for individual enterprise has existed for such a length of time that it has come to be regarded by many persons as competent under existing law, and while in my opinion such a construction is a perversion of the spirit of the law, I have heretofore treated it as permissable, and in inveighing against it scarcely a month ago used this language in addressing the Legislative Assembly:

"The organization of corporations to carry on large enterprises has become a necessity in this and other States; the development of our resources, and the carrying forward of projects for the public good, in many instances, are of such magnitude, and require the outlay of such large sums of money, that private capital cannot be induced to embark in them. The law should provide for the incorporation of such, but I condemn as bad legislation the existing statute, inherited from the Territory, which permits almost every character of business and industry to become the subject of an incorporation, whereby the liability of the stockholders is limited. No one but a creditor is entitled to see the books of the incorporation, and hence a person dealing with such concern in the first instance is at a disadvantage."

These remarks were directed against the propriety of permitting the very concerns, mercantile establishments, which this bill proposes to become the subject of an incorporation. If under the present law mercantile business may not be incorporated, I certainly cannot, in view of the opinion then and now entertained, approve the passage of a law which expressly creates the evil complained of.

Corporations are created to serve good purposes, and in many instances perform offices of public benefits and necessity that individuals would not, or could not accomplish, and if such are not already provided for, they should be. It is not intended, however, that corporations should usurp or supplant the functions of a citizen, or relieve him of personal responsibility in the ordinary avocations of life. Nor is it promotive of the common weal that they should. Public policy and expediency will not sanction it. If I were to set out deliberately to promote the formation of trusts and combinations in the necessaries of life by controlling the prices of such commodities, the first step taken in that direction would be to authorize mercantile establishments to incorporate. We are building for the future, and it will not be prudent for us to be unmindful of the fact that there is danger in the centralizing tendencies of business, and in the growth of monopolies and trusts which fortify themselves by the aggregation of capital, and by other influences permeating all branches of trade and classes of society. Unchecked by any feeling of individual responsibility, moved solely by a love of gain, unfettered by the duties of citizenship, they are enabled to perpetuate themselves by the adoption of methods and the use of agents which often scruple at no means to accomplish their ends. The result is the crowding out of healthy competition and the survival of the strongest which, under this process, is by no means the fittest. This result blunts the sensibilities of the citizen, builds up and fosters classes among the people, and undermines the fundamental principles upon which the governmental fabric is based.

If the right to incorporate business enterprises to the extent proposed by this bill for mercantile and other pursuits are carried into the field of agriculture, the result will be that large bodies of land will be owned by incorporated companies and tilled by tenantry.

The ownership would not then be vested in him who cultivated the land; the home, if preserved, would be less dear to him who occupied it; the best incentive to good citizenship would thereby be eradicated, and patriotism would be subdued, if not extinguished.

And again the effect of section 3 will be to put it in the power of those holding two-thirds of the stock of an existing incorporation to continue the corporation thirty years beyond the time of the original corporation, against the consent of the other stockholders, who may have sufficient reasons for winding up the affairs of the concern at the time when it would have expired by operation of law. It is but fair to presume that the stockholders have embarked in such enterprises with reference to the law as it existed at the time of the incorporation ; namely that it should continue for a period not exceeding twenty years, and the least of these should not be precipitated by the law into thirty years more of corporate control against his consent. Indeed this cannot be done without violating the plain constitutional provision against impairing the obligation of a contract.

The principle is elemental and the authorities are numerous to the effect that a State cannot in any manner alter the mutual relationship among the members of a corporation, or their relative rights and duties as established by their voluntary agreement when the company was formed. Thus, a law purporting to authorize the majority to extend or alter the business of a corporation against the will of a minority would be unconstitutional, although it contained a grant of new franchises to the corporators, and no existing franchises be thereby impaired.

Morawetz on Private Corporations. Sec. 1059, and cases cited.

The present bill not only authorizes an entire change in the business upon a two-thirds vote of the shareholders, but extends the time against the consent of the minority. This cannot be done without the unanimous consent of stockholders. Morawetz on Private Corporations. Sections 1060, 1083, 1047 and 645.

"It is evident that a State may authorize a corporation to alter its original enterprise and exercise new franchises to any extent without impairing any contract between the State and the corporators, or the agreement among the corporators themselves. The effect of such a law is merely permissive ; it enables the corporation to exercise new powers without breach of the law, but it takes no existing power, and effect no existing right. Whether the new franchises shall be exercised would depend wholly upon the corporation itself. Neither the majority of the shareholders nor any of the agents of the company would be entitled to exercise these franchises, *unless authorized to do so, either through the original charter contract, or the subsequent unanimous consent of the shareholders.*" Sec. 1083, *supra*.

But this appears to be of doubtful constitutionality in another point of view.

The constitution prohibits the granting of perpetuities except for charitable purposes.

If the Legislative Assembly can extend the term of a corporation now existing for thirty years, there is no reason why, before the expiration of the charter thus extended, another Legislative Assembly might not extend that for fifty years, and so on *ad infinitum*. It is due to the State and the minority stockholders that there should be a day of reckoning, and if the concern desires to continue business there is no reason why it cannot reorganize and pay into the treasury the fees for such privilege.

JOS. K. TOOLE,
Governor.

Arbor Day Proclamation.

Pursuant to law, and in keeping with the best interests of the State, I, Joseph K. Toole, Governor of the State of Montana, do hereby set apart the third Tuesday of April, (being the 15th day of April, 1890,) as a day for the planting of trees, beautifying homes, cemeteries, highways, public grounds and landscapes.

The observance of this day, aside from becoming a custom, beautiful in itself, will rapidly and materially enhance the value of all property so improved.

I, therefore, earnestly request that all people of Montana observe this day in the manner above indicated and I especially recommend that the attention of pupils in all of our schools be directed to the importance of the cultivation and preservation of trees and that whenever practicable they participate in planting trees, shrubs and vines in the school house grounds.

To those who desire to avail themselves of the more substantial rewards of exemption from taxation, attention is called to the following sections of an Act approved Sept. 15th, 1887.

"Sec. 3. Any person who is a resident of this Territory (State), who has now planted, or who shall hereafter plant and suitably cultivate for two years, one or more acres of land in fruit trees, he shall for the eight years following, thereafter, receive annually a reduction or exemption from his assessment of one hundred dollars for each acre so planted; provided, that the trees so planted shall not stand more than thirty-three feet apart, and are so long kept in a growing condition."

"Sec. 6. That when any resident of the Territory (State) has or may hereafter plant or cultivate for two years, a line of forest trees or fruit trees, not less than sixteen feet apart and not more than eight feet from any water ditches within his land, said land shall be exempt from taxation to the amount of one dollar annually thereafter on the assessed valuation of such land for each growing tree thereon for a period of five years."

IN WITNESS WHEREOF. I have hereunto set my hand and caused the great Seal of the State to be affixed.

[Seal.] Done at Helena, the Capital of said State this 8th day of March, in the year of our Lord, one thousand eight hundred and ninety.

JOS. K. TOOLE.

By the Governor:
L. ROTWITT,
Secretary of State.

Cattle Quarantine Proclamation.

THE STATE OF MONTANA, } SS.
EXECUTIVE OFFICE. }

HELENA, June 12, 1890.

Whereas, by virtue of and in pursuance of an Act of the Legislative Assembly of the Territory of Montana, entitled: "An Act to suppress and prevent the dissemination of contagious and infectious diseases among domestic and Texas cattle," approved March 10, 1885, it is my duty when I have reason to believe that any contagious or infectious disease has become epidemic in certain localities, by proclamation, to schedule such localities and to prohibit the importation from them of any live stock to this State except under such restrictions as I, after consultation with the State Veterinarian, may deem proper, and

Whereas. I have reason to believe, upon the representation of the Board of Stock Commissioners, and the State Veterinary Surgeon, that conditions exist which render domestic animals and Texas cattle in any and all of the following States and Territories, viz: New York, New Jersey, and Texas, liable to convey disease;

Now, therefore, I, Joseph K. Toole, Governor of the State Montana, by virtue of the authority conferred upon me by said Statute, and pursuant to the terms thereof, do hereby schedule the localities hereinbefore named, and I do hereby strictly forbid the importation into this State of any cattle whatsoever, which may have been brought from any portion of said scheduled localities, or any of them, except upon the certificate of the State Veterinary Surgeon that such cattle have been subjected to a quarantine of ninety days, and except Texas cattle that have been driven overland all the way from Texas and excepting also such cattle from said State of Texas as have been ninety days or more north or west of the following line, and which are accompanied with satisfactory certificates showing the fact:

Beginning at a point in the Indian Territory where the Thirty-sixth parallel of north latitude crosses the Arkansas river; thence southwest to the northeast corner of Wilbarger County, Texas; thence south along the east lines of Wilbarger, Taylor, Thockmorton, and Shackelford Counties; thence west along the south line of Shackelford County; thence south along the east lines of Taylor, Runnels and Concho Counties; thence west along the south line of Concho County; thence south along the east lines of Schleicher and Sutton Counties; thence west along the south lines of Sutton and Crockett Counties; thence south along the east line of Pecos County to the Rio Grande river.

And I do further forbid the importation into this State of any cattle driven or shipped from any other State, Territory or country, unless the same shall be accompanied by a certificate of health by the Veterinary Surgeon of said State, Territory or country, or his regularly appointed and authorized deputy, who shall have carefully examined all such cattle immediately prior to the giving of such certificate, or where this is impracticable, then said cattle shall be accompanied with such affidavits as shall satisfy the State Veterinary Surgeon that they have not been, for a period of ninety days, within the limits of the above scheduled districts; and all cattle, upon arrival in the State shall be examined at such station or stations as shall be designated by the State Veterinary Surgeon; provided, however, that nothing herein contained shall be so construed as to prohibit the transportation by rail through this State of any cattle destined for another State or Territory, and which are not unloaded within the limits of this State.

And I hereby warn all persons, corporations and companies whatsoever, not in any manner to violate, or attempt to violate, the prohibitions herein contained, or contained in said Act.

And I do hereby direct all Sheriffs, Constables, Stock Inspectors and other peace officers within this State to keep strict watch and to be vigilant and to see to it that all the commands of this, my proclamation, are obeyed and respected, and to arrest any and all persons violating the same. And I further direct all officers to report to me without delay all such violations of this, my proclamation.

And I do hereby revoke all previous proclamations respecting the importation of cattle into this State.

IN WITNESS WHEREOF, I have hereunto set my hand and caused the Seal of the State of Montana to be attached, at the City of Helena, the Capital of said State this 12th day of June, in the year of our Lord, eighteen hundred and ninety.

[Seal.]

JOS. K. TOOLE.

By the Governor:
L. ROTWITT,
Secretary of Montana.

Thanksgiving Proclamation.

STATE OF MONTANA, } ss.
EXECUTIVE OFFICE. }

WHEREAS, The President of the United States has appointed Thursday, the twenty-seventh day of November, to be observed as a day of prayer and thanksgiving; and

WHEREAS, This custom has come to be a part of the institutions of our country and is worthy of universal observance and respect,

THEREFORE, I, Joseph K. Toole, Governor of the State of Montana, do hereby direct public attention to the proclamation of the Chief Magistrate of this Republic and earnestly urge them to suspend all labor upon that day and at their homes and places of worship acknowledge their gratitude to Almighty God for the blessings of liberty, the advantages of State government, the continuance of life and generally for all the blessings vouchsafed unto us. On that day let the rich remember the poor; the strong help the weak and the citizen entertain the stranger.

[Seal.] IN TESTIMONY WHEREOF, I have hereunto set my hand and caused the Seal of the State of Montana to be affixed. Done at the City of Helena, this 10th day of November, A. D., one thousand eight hundred and ninety and the Independence of the United States the one hundred and fifteenth.   JOS. K. TOOLE.

By the Governor:
L. ROTWITT,
Secretary of State.

Arbor Day Proclamation.

THE STATE OF MONTANA, } ss.
EXECUTIVE OFFICE. }

HELENA, April 11, 1891.

In compliance with the law of the State, I, Joseph K. Toole, Governor of the State of Montana, do hereby set apart Tuesday, the 21st day of April, A. D. 1891, as a day for the planting of trees, beautifying homes, cemeteries, highways, public grounds, and landscapes; and those who teach in public schools are earnestly requested to direct and train the thoughts of the youth in tree planting and decorating by the practical observance of that day.

[Seal.] IN TESTIMONY WHEREOF, I have hereunto set my hand and caused the great seal of the State to be affixed at my office this 11th day of April, A. D. 1891.

JOS. K. TOOLE.
Governor.

By the Governor:
L. ROTWITT,
Secretary of State.

Quarantine Proclamation.

STATE OF MONTANA, } ss.
EXECUTIVE OFFICE.   }

WHEREAS, By virtue of and in pursuance of an Act of the Legislative Assembly of the Territory of Montana, entitled: "An act to suppress and prevent the dissemination of contagious and infectious diseases among domestic animals and Texas cattle," approved March 10, 1885, it is my duty, when I have reason to believe that any contagious or infectious disease has become epidemic in certain localities, by proclamation, to schedule such localities and prohibit the importation from them of any livestock to this State, except under such restrictions as I, after consultation with the State Veterinarian, may deem proper; and

WHEREAS, I have reason to believe, upon the representation of the Board of Stock Commissioners and the State Veterinarian, that conditions exist which render the cattle in certain portions of the State of Texas and the Indian Territory liable to convey disease.

NOW, THEREFORE, I, Joseph K. Toole, Governor of the State of Montana, by virtue of the authority conferred upon me by said statute and pursuant to the terms thereof, do hereby prohibit the importation, between the last day of March and the first day of November of all cattle from the State of Texas and Indian Territory, except such cattle as have been driven overland all the way or which shall show by satisfactory affidavits that they have been at least ninety days north of the 36th parallel of north latitude or west of a line drawn from the point where the 36th parallel of north latitude crosses the Arkansas River, southwest to the northeast corner of Wilbarger County, Texas; thence south along the east lines of Wilbarger, Taylor, Throckmorton and Shackelford Counties; thence west along the south line of Shackelford County; thence south along the east lines of Taylor, Runnels, Concho, Menard and Kimble Counties; thence west along the south lines of Kimble, Sutton and Crockett Counties; thence south along the east line of Pecos County to the Rio Grande River; and in default of such affidavits, such cattle will be deemed liable to convey Texas or Splenic fever, and will be held in quarantine at the risk and expense of the owner for not more than ninety days.

And I do further forbid the importation into this State of any cattle whatsoever driven or shipped from any other State, Territory or country, unless the same shall be accompanied by a certificate of health, given by the Veterinary Surgeon of said State, Territory or country, or his regularly appointed and authorized deputy, or where this is impracticable, then said cattle shall be accompanied with such affidavits as shall satisfy the State Veterinary Surgeon that they have not been, for a period of ninety days, within the limits of the above scheduled districts, and all cattle upon arrival in this State shall be examined at such station or stations as shall be designated by the State Veterinary Surgeon; *provided*, however, that nothing herein contained shall be so construed as to prohibit the transportation, by rail, through this State, of any cattle destined for any other State or Territory, and which are not unloaded within the limits of this State.

And I do hereby warn all persons, corporations and companies whatsoever not in any manner to violate or attempt to violate the provisions herein contained or contained in this act.

And I do hereby direct all sheriffs, constables, stock inspectors and other peace officers within this State to keep strict watch and to be vigilant and to see to it that all the commands of this, my proclamation, are obeyed and respected, and to arrest any and all persons violating the same; and I do hereby further direct all officers to report to me without delay all such violations of this, my proclamation.

And all former proclamations or parts thereof, in conflict with these provisions, are hereby revoked.

[Seal.]

IN TESTIMONY WHEREOF, I have hereunto set my hand and caused the seal of the State of Montana to be attached, at the city of Helena, the capital of said State, this 13th of April, 1891.

By the Governor: JOS. K. TOOLE.
L. ROTWITT,
Secretary of State.

Thanksgiving Proclamation.

STATE OF MONTANA, } ss.
EXECUTIVE OFFICE. }

HELENA, Nov. 14, 1891.

The second year of Statehood has filled the full measure of prophecy. From every source comes the glad news of prosperity and contentment. Every business interest has increased with the years. Mines and mills are in full blast. Stock and range are prepared to challenge the winter. Agriculture, made certain of maturity and prolific of yield by irrigation, is opening a new field for capital and labor. Our people are generally employed, and Government is felt, if at all, most in its benefits and least in its restraints. These are ample to demamd our recognition of Divine favor and to call for a day of thanksgiving and prayer.

Now, therefore, I, Joseph K. Toole, Governor of Montana, do accordingly appoint as such, Thursday, November 26th, A. D. 1891.

[SEAL.]

IN WITNESS WHEREOF, I have hereunto set my hand and caused the great seal of the State to be affixed. Done at the Capital, this fourteenth day of November, A. D. 1891.

By the Governor: JOS. K. TOOLE.
L. ROTWITT,
Secretary of State.

Irrigation Congress.

THE STATE OF MONTANA, } ss.
EXECUTIVE OFFICE.

HELENA, MONTANA, Dec. 12, 1891.

WHEREAS, The Irrigation Congress which lately met at Salt Lake City, Utah, adopted the following platform:

Resolved, That this Congress is in favor of granting in trust, upon such conditions as may serve the public interest, to the States and Territories needful of irrigation, all lands now a part of the public domain within such States and Territories, excepting mineral lands, for the purpose of developing irrigation, to render the lands now arid and fertile and capable of supporting a population.

Resolved, That it is the sense of this convention that the committee selected to propose and present to Congress the memorial of this convention respecting public lands, should ask as a preliminary to the cession of all the lands in the Territories in accordance with the resolutions of the convention, a liberal grant to said Territories and the States to be formed therefrom, of the public lands to be devoted to public school purposes.

WHEREAS, Large areas of arid lands and semi-arid lands, situated upon the great plains in the Dakotas, Western Nebraska, Kansas and Oklahoma were settled upon in good faith, by homeseekers, under the supposition that they were entering agricultural lands, and

WHEREAS, The settlers upon such lands have expended much time and money upon the same, and paid into the United States treasury therefor millions of dollars, only to discover that irrigation, to a greater or less extent, is necessary in making homes for themselves thereon; therefore, be it

Resolved, That the representatives of all the States and Territories directly interested in irrigation, do hereby pledge their unwavering support to the just demands of such settlers, that the general government shall donate at least a portion of the funds received from the sale of such lands toward the procurement of the means necessary for their irrigation.

Resolved, That this Congress heartily endorse the irrigation work of the Agricultural Department of the National Government in the collection and dissemination of information, especially its admirable progress reports covering the whole field of irrigation development, and that it favors large appropriations for this work hereafter; and,

WHEREAS, It is deemed advisable to obtain a direct expression of the people of this State upon the resolutions aforesaid; now, therefore, for that purpose and to that end, a convention is hereby called to meet at the City of Helena, on Thursday, January 7, 1892, at 12 o'clock M. The apportionment of delegates has been made as follows:

```
Beaverhead..................................  6
Choteau.....................................  4
```

Custer.................................... 4
Cascade................................. 10
Dawson.................................. 2
Deer Lodge.............................. 28
Fergus................................... 6
Gallatin.................................. 8
Jefferson................................ 10
Lewis and Clarke........................ 26
Meagher................................. 8
Missoula................................ 22
Madison................................. 8
Park..................................... 8
Silver Bow.............................. 40
Yellowstone............................. 4

Total............................... 144

The Boards of County Commissioners of the several counties are earnestly requested to appoint delegates at their December meeting according to the foregoing apportionment, based upon two delegates to each three hundred voters.

[Seal.]   By the Governor: JOS. K. TOOLE.
Attest:
    L. ROTWITT,
        Secretary of State.

Russian Famine Relief Proclamation.

WHEREAS, It has come to my notice that the peasantry of Russia, embracing a population of twenty-five millions of people, are now suffering from famine; and

WHEREAS, The only means of relief seems to rest with the generosity of the people; and

WHEREAS, The people of Montana are blessed with abundance and prosperity,

NOW, THEREFORE, I, JOSEPH K. TOOLE, Governor of said State, believing that the people of Montana are ever ready to respond to the just demands of humanity wherever found, and in answer to the appeal of the Russian Famine Relief Committee, do hereby recommend prompt and generous contributions.

And I further suggest and request all citizens, societies, committees and agencies desiring to aid in this work to put themselves in communication with said relief committee, at No. 734 Fourteenth street, Washington, D. C., which I am assured is acting in full harmony with The American National Red Cross Association, which associations have arranged for the prompt and expeditious transportation and distribution of all supplies received.

[Seal]   Given under my hand and the great Seal of the State of Montana, this eleventh day of February, in the year of our Lord, one thousand eight hundred and ninety-two.   JOS. K. TOOLE.
By the Governor:
    L. ROTWITT,
        Secretary of State.

Supplementing Russian Famine Relief Fund Proclamation.

STATE OF MONTANA, ⎱ ss.
EXECUTIVE OFFICE. ⎰

HELENA, March 25th, 1892.

WHEREAS, By a former Proclamation the people of this State were requested to contribute to the relief of the sufferers from famine in Russia, and

WHEREAS, The cause which impelled such action still exists, and

WHEREAS, The Provisional Department President of the Women's Relief Corps. Auxiliary to the Grand Army of the Republic, having advised me that said organization has six regularly established corps in Montana which are willing to assist in relieving the distress of the famine-stricken peasants of Russia.

Now, therefore, I do proclaim to the people of this State, and especially to those who may be willing to contribute to the relief of the suffering millions in Russia, that contributions for this purpose in money, may be sent to Mrs. Isabella Kirkendall, Provisional Department, President W. R. C., 407 Madison Avenue, Helena, Montana, and that all money so sent will be promptly remitted to the Russian Famine Relief Committee at Washington, D. C.

[SEAL.]   Given under my hand and the great seal of the State, this 25th day of March, A. D. 1892.

By the Governor: J. K. TOOLE.
   L. ROTWITT,
      Secretary of State.

Arbor Day Proclamation.

STATE OF MONTANA, ⎱ ss.
EXECUTIVE OFFICE. ⎰

HELENA, March 4, 1892.

Tuesday, the 19th day of April, A. D. 1892, is hereby set apart as a day for the planting of trees, beautifying homes, cemeteries, highways, public grounds and landscapes, and those who teach in public schools are especially requested to direct and train the thoughts of the youth in tree planting and decorating by the practical observance of that day.

[Seal.]   IN TESTIMONY WHEREOF, I have hereunto set my hand and caused the seal of the State to be affixed at the city of Helena, the capital of the said State, this fourth day of March, A. D. 1892.

                                     JOS. K. TOOLE.

By the Governor:
   L. ROTWITT,
      Secretary of State.

Flood Sufferers' Proclamation.

STATE OF MONTANA. } ss.
EXECUTIVE OFFICE. }

HELENA, May 24th, 1892.

WHEREAS, My attention has been directed to the loss of life and property by recent floods, extending from Sioux City, Ia., to the mouth of the Mississippi river, and the consequent suffering of many people; and,

WHEREAS, It has been proposed to formulate some plan of relief for those who require it,

Now, therefore, I do proclaim to the people of Montana that Dr. C. B. Miller, Charles D. Curtis, T. H. Kleinschmidt and Dr. C. K. Cole, of the City of Helena, have been by me appointed a committee, with full power to receive and forward for distribution such moneys and supplies as the people of this State may be willing to contribute to the suffering people in the flooded districts.

[SEAL.] Given under my hand the great seal of the State this 24th day of May, A. D. 1892.

By the Governor: JOS. K. TOOLE.
L. ROTWITT,
   Secretary of State.

Quarantine Proclamation.

STATE OF MONTANA. } ss.
EXECUTIVE DEPARTMENT. }

HELENA, June 24, 1892.

WHEREAS, Under the provisions of an Act of the Legislative Assembly of the State of Montana, entitled: "An Act to provide for the appointment of Deputy Veterinary Surgeons, and to suppress and prevent dissemination of scab and contagious diseases among sheep," approved March 14th 1889, it is made my duty whenever I shall have good reason to believe that any disease covered by this Act has become epidemic in certain locations in any other State or Territory, or that conditions exist that render sheep liable to convey disease, I shall thereupon by proclamation schedule such localities and prohibit the importation from them of any sheep into this State, except under such restrictions as I, after consultation with the veterinary surgeon, may deem proper; and

WHEREAS, I have reasons to believe that conditions exist which render sheep in any and all of the States of Oregon, Nevada, California Washington, Wyoming and Idaho, and the Territory of Utah, if brought into this state, liable to bring with them the disease known as Scab, and other loathsome contagious disorders,

NOW THEREFORE, I, JOS. K. TOOLE, Governor of the State of Montana, in obedience to the duly imposed upon me by said Statute and the terms thereof, do hereby schedule the localities hereinafter named, and I do hereby forbid the importation into the State of Montana of any sheep whatsoever which have been brought from any portion of said scheduled localities or any of them, except on the certificate of the State Veterinarian, or his duly authorized deputy, that such sheep have been inspected or have been found to be free from scab or any infections or contagious disease.

And I do hereby warn all corporations, persons and companies to give due and full notice to the State Veterinary Surgeon of Montana, preceding the arrival at the boundary line of said State of Montana, of all such sheep as come within the provisions of this proclamation, provided, however, that nothing in this proclamation shall be so construed as to prohibit the transportation of any sheep through this State by rail, and which sheep do not unload within said State.

IN WITNESS WHEREOF, I have hereto set my hand and caused the great Seal of the State of Montana to be affixed at the city of Helena, the capital of said State this fourteenth day of June, A. D. eighteen hundred and ninety-two.

[Seal.]

JOS. K. TOOLE.

By the Governor:
L. ROTWITT,
Secretary of State.

Permit for Sons of Veterans to Bear Arms.

EXECUTIVE OFFICE, }
HELENA, MONTANA. }

Upon the application of W. S. Votaw, Captain Commanding U. S. Grant Camp No. 1, Division of Montana, S. O. V., permission is hereby granted to the members of the order attending and participating in the exercises, parades and drills of the 11th Annual Encampment of the Commandery in-Chief, Sons of Veterans, U. S. A., to be held in the City of Helena, beginning August 8, 1892, to bear arms during the time they remain in this State, not exceeding thirty days.

IN WITNESS WHEREOF, I have hereunto set my hand and caused to be affixed the great seal of the State. Done at Helena, the capital of said State, the 22d day of June, A. D. 1892, and of the Independence of the United States the one hundred and sixteenth.

[Seal.]

JOS. K. TOOLE.

By the Governor:
L. ROTWITT,
Secretary of State.

Columbus Day Proclamation.

STATE OF MONTANA. } ss:
EXECUTIVE OFFICE. }

HELENA, Aug. 23, 1892.

WHEREAS, At the instance of the Executive Committee of the National Public Schools of Columbus Day, Congress has enacted a law instructing the President of the United States to issue a proclamation making Columbus Day a general holiday; and

WHEREAS, It is especially desirable that the Children of the land should observe the anniversary marking the date of the discovery by Columbus; and

WHEREAS, The World's Congress Auxiliary of the World's Columbian Exposition has made a patriotic suggestion that at the time that the Exposition grounds at Chicago are being dedicated, on October 21, 1892, the anniversary of the discovery of America, all the people of the United States unite in a celebration of the anniversary, of which celebration the public schools of the Republic be everywhere the center, as evidenced by the following resolution, passed by that body, viz:

"*Resolved*, That the Department of Superintendency of the National Educational Association heartily endorse this suggestion, as serving the purposes both of interesting the youth of the Republic in the Exposition, and also in giving to the public schools of the nation a fitting prominence as the fruit of four centuries of American life."

Now, therefore, I, Joseph K. Toole, Governor of the State of Montana, in accordance with the foregoing resolution, which was adopted, and the Act of Congress mentioned, do hereby designate and appoint Columbus Day, to-wit: October 21, 1892, as a public holiday, and recommend that it be observed at the different school houses within this State, and that civil and military organizations take part in the celebration.

The time is opportune to read again the history of our country. Every line of it speaks of a splendid civilization and records unparalleled achievements. Every man, woman and child who reads it and enters into the spirit of the occasion will find new incentives to transmit unimpaired to posterity the institutions bequeathed to us by our ancestors.

This work is especially committed to Hon. John Gannon, Superintendent of Public Instruction, and to the Montana Board of Lady Managers for the World's Fair Columbian Exposition.

IN TESTIMONY WHEREOF, I have hereunto set my hand and caused the great seal of Montana to be affixed at Helena, the Capital of said State, this 23rd day of August, A. D. 1892.

[SEAL.]

By the Governor:
    L. ROTWITT,
        Secretary of State.

JOSEPH K. TOOLE.

Labor Day Proclamation.

THE STATE OF MONTANA, ⎰ ss.
EXECUTIVE OFFICE. ⎱

HELENA, Aug. 30, 1892.

WHEREAS, by an Act approved March 4, 1891, it is provided that the first Monday of September in each year shall be set apart and declared to be a legal holiday to be known and designated as "Labor Day," and

WHEREAS, the people for whose direct benefit "Labor Day" was created are desirous of making the day a general holiday as contemplated by law.

NOW, THEREFORE, I, Joseph K. Toole, Governor of the State of Montana, do hereby recommend that Monday, Sept. 5, 1892, be observed as a general holiday.

It is suggested that business generally be suspended on that day as far as practicable, thereby giving to the friends and patrons of the day the largest freedom to enter into the spirit and enjoyment of the occasion.

[Seal.]

IN TESTIMONY WHEREOF, I have hereunto set my hand and caused the great seal of the State of Montana to be affixed at Helena, the 30th day of August, A. D. 1892.

JOS. K. TOOLE.

By the Governor:
L. ROTWITT.
Secretary of State.

Thanksgiving Proclamation.

THE STATE OF MONTANA, ⎰ ss.
EXECUTIVE OFFICE. ⎱

HELENA, November 9, 1892.

WHEREAS, the President of the United States has appointed Thursday, November the twenty-fourth, as a day of thanksgiving; and

WHEREAS, we have abundant reasons for observing a custom so long established.

NOW, THEREFORE, I, JOSEPH K. TOOLE, Governor of the State of Montana, do hereby recommend that on that day labor generally be suspended and that every one in his own way and according to his own convictions, make a proper acknowledgment to the Creator of the World for all that he possesses or enjoys, and forget not, wherever you can, to alleviate the suffering of the sick and lend a helping hand to the poor.

[Seal.] IN TESTIMONY WHEREOF, I have hereunto set my hand and caused to be affixed the great Seal of the State of Montana. Done at the City of Helena, the Capital of the said State of Montana, this ninth day of November. A. D., one thousand eight hundred and ninety-two.

By the Governor: JOS. K. TOOLE.
L. ROTWITT.
Secretary of State.

Correspondence Relating to the Exclusion of Chinese.

EXECUTIVE OFFICE, } ss.
HELENA, MONTANA. }

HELENA, Dec. 6. 1891.

Hon. Charles Foster Secretary of the Treasury, Washington, D. C.

Sir:— "I have the honor to represent that information is abundant to show that violations of the Act entitled 'An act to prohibit the coming of Chinese laborers to the United States,' approved Sept. 18, 1888, are of frequent occurrence along the boundary line between the United States and the Northwest Territory, and especially at points where the northern line of the State of Montana bounds the Northwest Territory.

I have reason to believe that there is an organized gang engaged in secretly introducing these unlawful immigrants into this State with headquarters along the line of the Canadian Pacific railroad. The sparsely settled section of country contiguous to our northern boundary makes our State a favorite dumping ground for Chinese who are the object of this illicit traffic.

For many years Chinese, in limited numbers, have resided in this State enjoying equal protection of the laws. Their presence in comparatively small numbers has excited no hostility against them in the past, but the constant and visible swelling of that population in the past year continues to be the subject of much agitation and severe criticism. I beg to assure you that this spirit of unrest and hostility which prevades certain sections of this State is not based upon a capricious or causeless change of sentiment concerning these people, but in good faith upon the notorious violation of a public statute.

I feel constrained, therefore, in behalf of the people of this State, to urge upon the United States a vigorous prosecution of all violations of the exclusion Act, and the prompt return to China of all persons who are here in violation of law.

If a corps of officers representing our government, possessing consummate courage, judgment, discretion and integrity, were distributed in convenient and proper places along the frontier, I believe that this gang of unlawful operators could be soon suppressed, and reasonable immunity from future complaint on that account be assured. I have the honor to be your obedient servant,
JOS. K. TOOLE,
Governor of Montana."

In answer to this the acting Secretary of the treasury department under date of Dec. 23, last, wrote: "I have the honor to acknowledge the receipt of your communication of the 6th instant, in relation to the unlawful introduction of Chinese into the United States, and in reply, to say that Special Agent J. J. Crowley, whose official address is St. Paul, Minn., will be directed to confer with you in relation to the subject as soon as the current business of his office will permit. Instructions have been sent to Agent Crowley, with the view to adoption of special measures to prohibit the traffic referred to."

DEPARTMENT OF STATE,
WASHINGTON, Feb. 8, 1892.

His Excellency, the Governor of Montana, Helena:
SIR: I have the honor to enclose a copy of a note of the *change ad interim* of China, here, relative to alleged oppressive treatment of his countrymen at Butte City, Montana.

It is trusted that a speedy and effective investigation will be made as to these alleged acts against Chinese, whose treaty-right of residence in this country does not appear to be in question.

I have the honor to be, Etc., Sir, your obedient servant,
JAMES G. BLAINE.

CHINESE LEGATION,
WASHINGTON, D. C.,
February 5, 1892.

Hon. James G. Blaine, Secretary of State:
SIR: I have the honor to inform you that from a report just received from the Imperial Chinese Consul General in San Francisco, I learn that various residents of Butte City, Montana, have been obstructing in their lawful business and outrageously treating the Chinese subjects in that place, which fact I feel constrained to bring to your notice in the hope that you will kindly cause prompt protection, as guaranteed by the treaty stipulations to be extended to them.

It appears that in the month of November last various labor unions of Butte City passed a regulation prohibiting the people in the said city against trading and dealing with the Chinese subjects resident there, and at the same time placed guards at the front of the Chinese stores to arrest and punish any native who should be found to infringe the regulation. Subsequently the labor unions forbade the native landlords to hire any more of their houses to the Chinese and ordered them to raise the rents of houses already tenanted by them. They further required the Chinese laundrymen to register their names and attempted to extort from them each ten dollars for the same. Upon their refusal to comply with their demand the lawless people fired at them and assaulted some of them about the head with their pistols, so grievously wounding them that their lives were in peril.

As the Chinese subjects resident in the United States are entitled to the protection of the laws of the country and guaranteed to them by Article 3, of the treaty of 1880 between China and the United States, I beg respectfully to solicit immediate relief on the part of the outraged Chinese of Butte City, and hope that the necessary instructions may be issued to the local authorities of the State of Montana to take prompt measures for the suppression of such illegal actions and outrages committed upon the Chinese subjects there. Accept, Sir, &c., PUNG KWANG YU.

Reply to the Request of Secretary Blaine to Investigate Alleged Chinese Outrages in Butte.

THE STATE OF MONTANA, /
EXECUTIVE OFFICE. \
HELENA, Feb. 26, 1892.
Hon. James G. Blaine, Secretary of State Washington, D. C.:

SIR—Further replying to your note of the 8th inst. with inclosure from the charge ad iterim of China, at Washington, specifying certain acts of oppression alleged to have been committed by the labor Unions of Butte City, in this State, upon his countrymen residing there, I have the honor to inform you that, accompanied and assisted by the Attorney General of Montana, I visited Butte City, and pursuant to your request, have investigated the alleged acts of oppression referred to as having occurred in November, 1891.

My investigation was public and exhaustive, and revealed the following state of affairs:

In the month of April, 1891, the health officer's report disclosed the fact that 841 Chinamen were residing in that city. In November, 1891, a census taken by direction of one of the labor organizations showed that the Chinese population had increased to 1,750, who were engaged in various occupations at wages below the current prices for the same kind of labor performed by other persons, and to the exclusion of other worthy people. Whereupon the labor organizations of Butte City instituted a "boycott" against the Chinese, but did not, in fact, make the same operative until January 1, 1892, since which time it has been observed by the members of such labor organizations. The effect of this "boycott" is to withdraw from the Chinese residing there all patronage of members of the various Unions, but in no instance has a labor union, directly or indirectly unsed force or violence respecting these people. Nor can it be shown that in any assault committed on Chinese, that the assailant was a member of a labor Union. Whatever may be said of the propriety of "boycotting" by means of which people, or a class of people, voluntarily withdraw their patronage from others, I know of no law in this State to prevent it. A person living under the protection of this State has a right to adopt and follow any lawful industrial pursuit not injurious to the community, which he may see fit, but we are too far removed in time and statesmanship from the age when governmental perfects assumed to supervise a large range of affairs long since, in all enlightened lands, regarded as outside of governmental functions, to acknowlenged a duty or obligation to patronize or support such person in his business or employment.

Not an instance was brought to my notice, nor do I believe that one can can be found, where force or violence was employed to enforce any demand of the Unions.

It is believed by the Chinamen with whom I talked that the "boycott" is effective, and that they cannot long stand out against it.

It is fair to say in this connection that the Chinese are not the only persons who are the objects of "boycotts" at Butte City, but that sundry merchants and other persons, without regard to nationality, are embraced within it, and so published to the world.

Nor do I think it proper to withhold from you the information that there appears to be no community of interests between the Chinese and these Unions: in fact the latter are emphatic in their opposition to their further admission into this country, and I may add that this feeling is general, and confined to no political party.

It is doubtless true that isolated cases of assaults upon Chinamen have occurred af Butte within the last three months. The persons committing the assaults belong to the criminal classes, and in nearly every instance were promptly arrested and punished. The court records show that during the present month four persons were tried, convicted and sentenced for offenses committed against the persons and property of Chinese.

I am confident that the charge of extorting money from Chinese laundrymen by force and violence grew out of the arrest of one Arthur Fowler on January 16, 1892, who entered a laundry demanded money, and in default of which fired at the keeper and beat him about the head with his pistol.

The most intelligent Chinaman whom I met in Butte, and who represented his countrymen in the investigation, told me that he knew of no other case where a similar demand was made, and that the Consul General at San Francisco, who formulated the complaint, had misunderstood the purport of the telegram sent him on the subject. Fowler has been in jail since his arrest, awaiting his trial at a regular term of court. He was, on the 18th inst., tried and convicted of the crime of assault with intent to kill, and sentenced to the State penitentiary for two years. I enclose a copy of the information, testimony and judgment for your inspection.

I know of no offense committed against the person or property of Chinese in that city where diligence has not been used to arrest the offenders.

The most recent case that has come to my attention is the burning of a Chinese laundry about ten days ago at Meaderville, a few miles distant from Butte. Warrants for the arrest of the guilty parties were immediately put into the hands of the sheriff of the county, who has made and is now making every endeavor to apprehend them, and in the event of a failure so to do, then I am assured that a special grand jury will be called, thereby affording ampler facilities to that end.

I enclose a letter from the sheriff of Silver Bow County, showing that no discrimination is made against Chinese in that county, but that they receive the same protection afforded other residents of the city and county.

Trusting that the foregoing report may be satisfactory to the charge ad interim of China, at Washington, and his countrymen, I have the honor to be   Your obedient servant,

JOS. K. TOOLE,
Governor of Montana.

Relating to the Strike in the Cœur d'Alene Country, and in re Peter Breen.

(*Telegram.*)

Lookout, Mont., July 19, 1892.

Gov. Toole, Helena, Mont.:

An armed lot of desperadoes are said to be in the vicinity and escaping from Shoshone County. Have we authority from you to pursue?

GEN. W. P. CARLIN,
4th Infty. Comdg. U. S. Troops,
J. F. CURTIS,
Col. Idaho Natl. Guards.

(*Telegram.*)

Helena, July 20, 1892.

Gen. W. P. Carlin, 4th Infty. Commanding U. S. Troops, and J. F. Curtis, Col. Idaho National Guards, Lookout, Montana:

Application for extradition of alleged fugitives from justice properly made by the Governor of Idaho will be promptly recognized. Consent for military authorities to pursue them in this State is refused.

JOS. K. TOOLE,
Governor of Montana.

THE STATE OF MONTANA,
Executive Office, Helena, July 21, 1892.

W. P. Carlin, Brig. Gen. Commanding U. S. Troops, and J. F. Curtis, Col. Idaho Nat'l. Guards:

Gentlemen: The bearer of this, Mr. Matthews, has presented to me the attached letters, which have satisfied me that his mission is loyal and humane, and one which I hope will protect him against unnecessary delay or obstruction in his purpose. I understand from him, as well as from the letters, referred to, that his object is solely to minister to the wants of the families of deceased and disabled persons lately in trouble in that part of Idaho now under martial law.

Such a worthy purpose I hope will meet with the approval of those in authority.

I have the honor to be with great respect,
Your obedient servant,
JOS. K. TOOLE.
Governor of Montana.

SILVER BOW CLUB, Butte City, Montana, July 20, 1892.

Hon. J. K. Toole, Governor Montana:

Dear Sir: This will be presented by Mr. Thomas Matthews. Mr. Matthews informs me that he desires to visit and administer to the relief of the distressed in the disturbed district of Idaho, and desires your endorsement that he may avoid trouble. I am satisfied that Mr. Matthews is a reliable gentleman and that his mission is one of humanity, and you will confer a special favor by giving what assistance is in your power.

Yours truly,
W. Y. PEMPERTON.

Butte City, Montana, July 20, 1892.

His Excellency, Gov., J. K. Toole, Helena, Montana:

Dear Governor: The bearer, Mr. Thos. Matthews, asks me for a letter of introduction to you. He will make known to you his business.

I have known Mr. Matthews for several years, as a good citizen, a member of our State militia, and altogether reliable. I believe what he may tell you respecting his business can be strictly relied upon as the absolute truth. I am, with great respect, yours very truly, J. E. RICKARDS.

MAGUIRE'S OPERA HOUSE, Butte, Mont., July 20, 1892.

Hon. Jos. K. Toole, Governor of Montana:

Your Excellency: The bearer, Thos. Matthews, is bent on a charitable mission to the Cœur d'Alene's, his desire being that a proper system of relief and distribution of provisions should be provided for families in distress. For this worthy object he has the good wishes of every one anxious in helping the furtherance of so humane a cause.

A favorable consideration by Your Excellency of Mr. Matthews and his efforts, can not be otherwise than productive of good results.

Yours most respectfully.
J. MAGUIRE.

D. J. HENNESY MERCANTILE CO.,
Butte City, Mont., July 20, 1892.

His Excellency, Gov. Jos. K. Toole, Helena, Montana:

This will introduce Mr. Thos. Matthews, who desires to proceed to the Cœur d'Alene on a mission which he himself will explain.

His mission as stated by him, is certainly a worthy one and should meet with no opposition.

So far as I know. Mr. Matthews is a thoroughly reliable man and his statements are entitled to full credence. Having been selected by the Butte Miners Union for this mission, is a sufficient guarantee of Mr. Matthews, without any further endorsements.

Yours respectfully,
D. J. HENNESSY.

HALL OF THE BUTTE MINER'S UNION.
Organized June 13, 1878.

Butte, Mont., July 19, 1892.

To His Excellency, J. K. Toole, Governor of Montana:

It was resolved this evening to send the bearer of this note to Idaho to look after provisions and property.

Trusting you will recommend the same to Gov. Wiley, also to Adjutant General Curtis in order that these gentlemen will be able to travel through the country without being arrested.

Faithfully yours,
JOSEPH THOMAS,
[Seal.] *President.*
THOMAS MALOUIN.
Recording Secretary.

Bearers: THOMAS MATTHEWS.
EUGENE E. KELLY.

In re Peter Breene, a Citizen of Montana Arrested in the State of Idaho.

HELENA, Aug. 22, 1892.

Hon. Norman B. Willey, Governor of Idaho, Boise, Idaho:

DEAR SIR—I have the honor to inform you that I am just in receipt of the following telegram:

Butte City, Mont. Aug. 14, 1892.

To Governor J. K. Toole:

DEAR SIR -As the Executive of Montana we appeal to you to see that justice will be done a Montana citizen incarcerated at Wallace, Idaho, Hon. Peter Breen. He is in solitary confinement in a dungeon that is filthy and without ventilation, and it is humanity's duty to see that justice will be accorded. No person is permitted to see him, the officers refuse to return the writs of his arrest to the proper officers so that action can be instituted to give him a hearing. The treatment of the prisoner is brutal and inhuman. We are ready to offer bail in ample amount for Breen when wanted. We appeal to your humanity as a man and to your duty to protect the rights belonging a citizen of Montana.

W. E. DEENEY,
President Silver Bow Trades and Labor Assembly.
C. W. COLEMAN,
Secretary Silver Bow Trades and Labor Assembly.
JOHN BROOKS,
M. W., L. of L., 2,330.
FRANK L. REBER,
M. W., Clerks Assembly.
F. LANGSTON,
President Carpenters Union, 112.
J. J. KNOWLTON,
President Workingmen's Union.
P. MEANEY,
Secretary Workingmen's Union.
W. H. EDDY,
F. Secretary Miner's Union.
JOSEPH THOMAS,
President Butte Miner's Union.
T. MALOUIN,
Secretary Butte Miner's Union.
EDWARD FRNACIS,
President Bricklayers and Masons' International Union.
JOHN GAEBLE,
R. S. D. A., 93, K. of L.
M. G'NEILL,
M. W., 3,918, K. of L.
DELIA MOORE,
M. W. L., Women's Protective Union.

I have no further information on the subject, but the charges being specific I feel obliged to ask you to investigate them, and if found true to take necessary steps to correct the abuses complained of. However grave the charges may be against the prisoner it is needless to inform you, that like all others, the presumption of innocence attends him until proven guilty. Believeing that you would not suffer or permit such conduct as alleged in the foregoing telegram to go unrebuked if brought to your attention, I have the honor to renew my request for a speedy investigation of the same, and to further request that all proper and usual facilities be accorded him to prepare for trial. I have the honor to be your obedient servant,

JOS. K. TOOLE,
Governor of Montana.

EXECUTIVE OFFICE. 77

Reply of Governor Willey.

STATE OF IDAHO, } ss.
EXECUTIVE DEPARTMENT. }

BOISE CITY, Idaho, Aug. 30, 1892.

Hon. J. K. Toole, Governor of Montana, Helena, Montana.

SIR:—I beg leave to enclose a copy of a communication just received from Captain Ballance for your further information in the matter of the treatment of Peter Breen as stated in your letter of the 15th instant.

Very respectfully,
NORMAN B. WILLEY.
Governor.

WALLACE, Idaho, Aug. 26, 1892.

His Excelllncy, Norman B. Willey, Governor of Idaho:

DEAR SIR:— In reply to your letter of Aug. 22, enclosing copy of letter from his excellency, the Governor of Montana, dated the 15th inst., concerning the treatment accorded Peter Breen, a citizen of Montana, in confinement at this place, I have the honor to state, as directed by Col. J. F. Curtis, who is now absent from the city, in regard to the statement:

1. "He is in solitary confinement in a dungeon that is filthy and without ventilation." That he is confined in a wooden cell, it is not in any sense of the word a dungeon, it is perfectly clean and properly ventilated.

2. "No man is permitted to see him." Proper facilities have been furnished him to see his attorneys, and others, having a legal right to see him. Threats having been made to rescue him, a high board fence was placed around the building and used as a jail, and proper measures taken to prevent unauthorized persons from having access to him and other prisoners, as a necessary precaution.

3. "The officers refuse to return the writs of his arrest to the proper officers, so that action can be instituted to give him a hearing." Mr. Breen's attorneys have been furnished with all proper facilities for communicating with him and have done so. No proper attempt was made by his attorneys to obtain a hearing for him until last Monday, it not being considered by them as desirable to do so. The matter is fully set forth in the enclosed newspaper clipping taken from the Anaconda Standard of August 19th, 1892, being a copy of a letter from the District Attorney, Fifth judicial district Idaho.

4. "The treatment of the prisoner is brutal and inhuman." The treatment awarded Mr. Breen has not at any time been brutal or inhuman. He is accorded the same treatment as accorded other prisoners under charge of the sheriff, which is proper in every respect.

"We are ready to offer bail in ample amount for the appearance of Breen when wanted." To be ready to offer bail, to offer efficient bail, and to give bail are very different things. Informal and irresponsible talk has been indulged in concerning the furnishing of bail, but no proper offer to give bail was made until yesterday. Twenty thousand dollars was the amount of bail fixed by the district judge, but up to the present writing his friends have been unable to procure it. Previous proceedings on the subject are set forth in the newspaper clipping heretofore mentioned. Before the receipt of your letter, measures had been taken to have the matter investigated by a board of impartial army officers, and I enclose herewith a copy of that report.

The matter was also investigated by Mr. Crossthwaite, an agent of the attorney general's office of the United States, who informed me that there was not in his opinion, any truth in the report of ill-treatment of any of the prisoners.

The county seat of this county is at Murray, the jail there is a very secure place, but Murray is inaccessible and the county prisoners are temporarily retained here in a frame building which was originally intended for a calaboose. The wooden cell where Mr. Breen is confined is undoubtedly more pleasant and better ventilated than would be one of the steel cells in the county jail at Murray.

All proper and usual facilities are and will be accredited to him to prepare for trial. I am, sir, very respectfully your obedient servant,

JOHN GREEN BALLANCE,
Captain 22nd Infantry, Asst. Judge Advocate General.

Reply of Silver Bow Trades and Labor Union to the Report of Governor Willey.

Butte, Montana, Sept. 10, 1892.

Gov. J. K. Toole, Helena, Mont.:

Dear Sir: The letter forwarded by the Executive of Idaho, in answer to the charges made by representatives of this body as to the treatment accorded Hon. Peter Breen, at Wallace, a general and positive denial is made to all the specifications involved.

The answer to this report, the Trades and Labor Assembly states, that the report as made to the governor of Idaho by the officer in question, is based upon an examination made after Mr. Breen had been removed from the filthy cell into which he had been placed at first, to one with better ventilation and accommodations; thus the report is in the nature of an ingenious whitewash and evasive in its particular application.

As a substantiation of this we need only refer you to some of the evidence produced before and the report made by the army officers who investigated the charges. This report, with some of the evidence, is published in the Cœur d'Alene *American*, of August 29, 1892. So much for this.

EXECUTIVE OFFICE.

The worst misrepresentation in this report is that which refers to the bail proposition. This report is not only a misrepresentation of the facts in the case, but is an unworthy attempt to bolster up an untair and unjustifiable position, as assumed by some of the Shoshone County authorities.

Legitimate bail was offered, every fair proposition made that could be made, consequently the friends of Breen did and have to-day $20,000 deposited with Larabie Bros. & Co. at Deer Lodge for the purpose of affording indemnification for Breen. The money is ready, and more, too, if a just disposition will be manifested to accord Peter Breen a proper opportunity to put up bail bonds. But this, according justice in the premises, does not seem to be an attribute of the officials in question, hence the failure so far of having Breen out of a prison cell to await his trial.

The County Clerk, who is only under nominal bonds, demanded that the money should be placed in his possession, irrespective of any safeguard to the parties who had furnished the money. These actions were of an arbitrary character and the demands such that it vitiated any fair, equitable basis of according legitimate action in the case.

In refutation to this misrepresentation that no bona fide proposition for bail was made, we herewith furnish copies of some of the letters and telegrams bearing on the features of the case, viz:

Deer Lodge, Aug. 22, 1892.

Cœur d'Alene Bank, Wallace, Idaho:

Peter Breen's friends have arranged with us and please obtain bonds in $20,000. We guarantee you against any loss; we confirm by letter.

LARABIE BROS. & CO.

Cœur d'Alene Bank, Wallace, Idaho:

Gentlemen: We wired you this morning as follows: "Peter Breen's friends have arranged with us, please obtain bonds in sum of $20,000. We guarantee you against any loss; we confirm by mail."

We hereby confirm same and will hold you or bondsmen harmless that secure it.

Thanking you in advance for this courtesy and trusting we may be able to fully reciprocate at some future time, we are,

Very truly yours,
LARABIE BROS. & Co.

The Wallace Bank, capitalized as it is only at $15,000, was not in the courtesy business, hence this attempt failed.

Other negotiations were then opened and an agent with power of attorney of the Deer Lodge bank sent to Wallace to perfect proper arrangements with parties. A certificate of deposit for $20,000 was forwarded, but this was not satisfactory; it was cold cash or negotiable paper that might be utilized or nothing with these officials.

The following telegrams from Larabie Bros. & Co. to agent substantiate this.

Deer Lodge, Aug. 28, 1892.
To Agent, Wallace, Idaho:
We mail you to day necessary papers with instructions. Wait for letter.
LARABIE BROS. & CO.

Deer Lodge, Aug. 29, 1892.
To Agent, Wallace, Idaho:
Telegrams received, following our instructions letter 28th. Endorsed certificate as collateral only and non-negotiable to third parties. Wire when arrangements completed.
LARABIE BROS. & CO.

Deer Lodge, Aug. 31.
To Agent, Wallace, Idaho:
Will deposit $20,000 with First National Bank, Helena, or Boise, Idaho, to order of court if prisoner not delivered. If not satisfactory, explain situation to Breen and come home. Court so unreasonable: can't do more: answer.
LARABIE BROS. & Co.

This constitutes only part of the attempt to accord satisfactory arrangements for Breen's bond. Nothing was of avail but cold cash or its equivalent in the hands of an official, only under nominal bonds. In view of this it is safe to say that, inasmuch, that this report is misleading and untruthful in this particular, it is untruthful in its entire denial.

In addition to the above, if the cash money had been placed in the hands of the County Clerk for Breen's appearance at trial, a cat-hop was arranged by some parties to immediately arrest them again on a different charge and thus if possible jeopardize the money involved.

This is from reliable authority, and we venture to say will not be disputed.

This will give you an idea of the methods employed in Shoshone county at present. A justice, as it would seem, with eyes blinded; a justice that needs commend itself to fair minded men. Does it not seem like mockery? Will that sense of fair play, supposed to afford any individual a fair hearing, stand idly by such a travesty and applaud it?

It would seem that this is sufficient to demonstrate that what is supposed to be the majesty of the law is not the ruling modicum in Northern Idaho, but the persecuted power of organized greed as represented by the Mine Owners' association.

Justice can hardly be expected at such hands, hence in the name of all fairness, we renew the charge that a Montana citizen is not granted decent justice in Idaho.

   SILVER BOW TRADES AND LABOR ASSEMBLY,
C. M. COLEMAN,   W. E. DEENEY,
 Secretary.   *President.*

Relating to British Indians Committing Depredations in Montana.

HELENA, Sept. 1, 1892.
Hon. S. B. Elkins, Secretary of War, Washington, D. C.

SIR—I have the honor to transmit, for your consideration, the enclosed correspondence relating to certain roving bands of Canadian Indians now in this State.

We have exhausted every means at our command to rid this State of these Indians, and now appeal to the United States, through the War Department, for relief.

The Canadian authorities have expressed the belief that if these Indians were escorted a time or two to the Northwest border they would discontinue their incursions into this State.

I have the honor, therefore, to ask that the War Department investigate the status of these Indians, and if found to be British subjects, that they be conveyed to their respective reservations, and that the proper authorities be requested to keep them within their own jurisdiction.

The character of these Indians, and their continued visitations to this country, to the annoyance and damage of our citizens, is set forth in one of the enclosures, addressed to the Hon. James G. Blaine, Secretary of State.

Hoping that you may find it proper and expedient to cause prompt investigation and action to be had, I have the honor to be,
Your obedient servant,
JOS. K. TOOLE,
Governor.

FORT BENTON, Mont., Feb. 3, 1891.
Gov. Joseph K. Toole, Helena, Mont:

DEAR SIR—Herewith I enclose article from Calgarry Herald. By next mail will enclose you article from River Press concerning same.

Would you do me the honor to advise if there has been any action taken about the Cree Indians, either by yourself, as Governor of the State, or by the United States authorities at your request or suggestion, which we would be at liberty to publish for the information of our people.

They are much interested in having these Indians put under charge of either one Government or the other. They want them taken from Northern Montana.
With much respect, etc.,
WM. H. TODD.

Are They Canadian Indians?

The Fort Benton River Press is exclaiming lustily against the "wandering Crees," whom it calls "Canadian Crees," and who are described as "scattered in camps throughout Northern Montana," with whom are "other thieving Indians from over the Canadian line, having places of refuge at convenient distances where they can go and get food to sustain them on their horse stealing expeditions." Again, certain home Crees are said to "act as pickets and chiefs of subsistence for other thieving Indians of their own flesh and blood just across the line in Canada." In another article it says that a band of 200 Indian bucks or more were encamped within 37 miles of Helena, and it alleges that they are "Canadian renegades from across the line who have been causing great alarm, and that Governor Toole will immediately call upon Secretary Blaine to request the Canadian Covernment to come down and take charge of their wards without delay." It speaks of "these roaming bands of Canadian Crees who have been traveling wherever their sweet will led them among the settlements and over the ranges of North Montana, a constant source of annoyance and trouble to our people, secretly killing cattle, setting fire to the ranges and engaging in petty thieving."

These are strong statements, and they are written in such terms as would leave the impression that there could be no doubt of these Indians being Canadian Indians, and that a call must be made on the Canadian Government to keep them at home. Now if these are Canadian Indians for whose conduct our Government is responsible, we ought to know it: but we are inclined to think that our Indian Department knows nothing of them. Still, in view of these repeated charges, enquiry should be made and steps taken to remedy any real grievance, if such be found to exist. That there is a doubt resting upon their classification as Canadian Indians by the River Press is shown by the following paragraph in the same article from which we have been quoting :

"We are pleased to note that Governor Toole has taken the matter in hand, and sincerely trust that he will give Secretary Blaine no rest until these Indians are taken and put upon a reservation and kept there either by Canada or the United States. If they are Canadian wards they should be sent across the line before a spell of hard weather comes and they are again thrown upon the charity of the state of Montana, as was the case in the winter of 1886-7. If they claim United States protection, and can make their claim good, then let our Government take charge of them, and put them on a reservation, and treat them just as it does other tribes of Indians. They should not be permitted to wander over the country, armed to the teeth, a meance and a terror to outlying settlements."

If it is discovered by the officials of the United States that these are Canadian and not United States Indians, our Government will soon be appraised of the fact from official sources. At present it is well known that all proper means have been taken on the Canadian side of the line to prevent the movement of Indians from one country into the other, and having regard to the charges made by the Benton Press, these precautions should not be relaxed. At the same time it will not surprise us to find that the Canadian Government has no responsibility in reference to the Indians who are complained of by the River Press, and who are probably American Indians who have not been properly looked after by the United States authorities. It is desirable that they should be dealt with by these authorities. if for no other reason than to stop the repetition of charges of neglect of duty on the part of our Indian Department.--*Calgary Herald.*

KALISPELL, Nov. 20. 1891.

Hon. H. J. Haskell, Attorney General, Helena, Montana:

DEAR SIR At the request of a number of citizens I bring to your notice a matter of considerable importance to residents of this portion of the State. That is in reference to renegade Indians that have crossed the border and pitched their tepees here for the winter. In addition to being an awful nuisance they are making an awful slaughter of game, which was plentiful in this region until their advent. The timber skirting the various streams of the valley is fairly alive with Crees. Chippewas and Kootenais. Whenever they can prevail upon some unscrupulous ginseller to give them liquor they hold high carnival. The Flathead Indians stay on their reservation and give no trouble. It is due to the large number of people who have made their homes in the valley that the attention of the Canadian authorities be called to this matter and a request made that they call their wards home. Trusting that this will receive attention I am, yours truly,

H. J. MOCK.

SILVER BOW, Mont., Aug. 27, 1892.

Hon. J. K. Toole, Helena:

DEAR SIR I desire to call your attention once more to those Cree Indians. We have them in our vicinity yet in goodly numbers. They left here about four weeks ago and went north; said they were going to Missoula, and we were in hopes they would work back to the boundary line, but on Tuesday last they returned, bringing all their relations with them, "I guess." Now. the result of last winter and spring's negotiations between Secretary Blaine and the Canadian authorities was favorable to their removal, and at the present time everything seems favorable. The people are more than favorable. They are camped at present about two miles west of Silver Bow Junction, and the indications are that they intend to tarry the coming winter with us, but we would rather excuse them. You may have heard from one or two of my neighbors concerning them. as I heard they proposed writing you; but as I had written you last winter, also Hon. T. C. Power and United States Attorney Weed, some of our people wished me to again call your attention to them.

Hoping you will take the necessary steps for their permanent removal, I remain, Yours very truly,

THOS. O. MILES.

THE STATE OF MONTANA, } SS.
EXECUTIVE OFFICE.

HELENA, Feb. 8, 1892.

Thos. O. Miles, Esq., Silver Bow, Mont.

DEAR SIR: I have your letter and petition relating to Cree Indians loitering near Silver Bow. The right to remove these Indians does not belong to me. I have repeatedly informed the State Department of this and similar intrusions by the Crees, but nothing has resulted from the correspondence. I am fully aware of the great annoyance these Indians give to small settlements, and how women and children are frightened by them, and if there was anything I could do without violating State or International law, to relieve this community of their presence I would gladly do it, but nothing remains to be done except to urge through Secretary of State Blaine the return of these Crees to their home in the N. W. Territory. Yours truly,

J. K. TOOLE.

THE STATE OF MONTANA, } SS.
EXECUTIVE OFFICE.

HELENA, February 8, 1892.

Hon. James G. Blaine, Secretary of State, Washington, D. C.

SIR:— I again have the honor to call your attention to a band of Cree Indians, wards of the Canadian Government, who are hanging about a small settlement in Silver Bow County, in this State, and to enclose papers concerning same.

These Indians are regarded as outlaws, and are a constant source of fear and annoyance to women and children in sparsely settled communities. They have no visible means of support. The belief is general that they plunder our people in the winter and return across the border in the spring.

This is not an exceptional occurrence, but I beg to assure you that it is systematically practiced and has been for many years. Bands of these Indians being in no less than four counties of this State at the present time.

Yours truly, JOS. K. TOOLE,
Governor.

THE STATE OF MONTANA, } SS.
EXECUTIVE OFFICE.

Hon. James G. Blaine, Secretary of State, Washington, D. C.

HELENA, Oct. 22, 1891.

SIR—I have the honor to transmit herewith a communication from Hon. Geo. O. Eaton, United States Surveyor General, respecting the depredations of certain Indians belonging to the jurisdiction of the Northwest Territory.

Our citizens are clamorous for redress against these depredations. Believing that a communication from your department might have the effect to prevent a recurrence of these depredations. and obviate arrests and trials. I have the honor to request that such action be taken in the premises as may seem to you proper and expedient.

JOS. K. TOOLE,
Governor.

LEWISTOWN. Aug. 31. 1892.
(*Received at Helena. Montana. 11:48 a. m.*)

To Governor Toole:

Twenty lodges of Canadian Cree Indians camped on Doe Creek last night. Traveling south. Killing game. Please remove them.

JAMES FERGUS.

DEPARTMENT OF STATE.

WASHINGTON, March 18, 1892.

His Excellency, the Governor of Montana, Helena:

Sir: With reference to your letter of October 22, 1891, in regard to the depredations of a band of Stony Indians from Canada. I have the honor to send you herewith enclosed, for your information. a copy of dispatch No. 168. from the Consul General at Ottawa. transmitting copies of the correspondence between the Consul General and the Dominion Authorities in the matter. In a certified copy of a report of a committee of the Privy Council, approved by the Governor General, regret is expressed for the occurrence, and the suggestion is made that if the Indians were turned back on one or two occasions by the American authorities, they would discontinue their excursions across the boundary line.

I have the honor to be, Sir, Your obedient servant.
WILLIAM T. WHARTON,
Acting Secretary.

Enclosure:

From the Consul General at Ottawa. No. 168, March 10, 1892, with enclosures.

BRITISH LEGATION.

WASHINGTON, April 6, 1892.

The Hon. James G. Blaine, Secretary of State:

SIR: With reference to my note of the 30th of January last. respecting the case of certain Cree Indians, who are stated to have wandered from the Northwest Territories of Canada, into Montana, I have the honor to enclose herewith a copy of an approved Minute of the Privy Council of Canada, embodying a report on the subject by the Canadian Superintendent General of Indian Affairs, which has been transmitted to me by the Governor General of Canada for communication to you.   I have the honor, etc.,

JULIAN PAUNCEFOTE.

Privy Council, Canada.

Certified copy of a report of a committee of the Honorable Privy Council, approved by His Excellency the Governor General in Council, on the 29th of March, 1892.

The Committee of the Privy Council have had under consideration a dispatch dated 28th January, 1892, from Her Majesty's Minister at Washington, enclosing a copy of a note, dated 26th January, 1892, received from the United States Government on the subject of certain Cree Indians, who are stated to have wandered across the boundary line from Northwest Territory of Canada into Montana.

The Superintendent General of Indian Affairs to whom the dispatch was referred states that a copy of the dispatch and enclosures were forwarded to the Indian Commissioner for Manitoba and the Northwest Territories for his report on the statements made therein, and a letter dated the 17th of March instant has been received from that office, in which he states that, with the exception of a few Indians who go for the purpose of visiting their friends in the United States and returning, nothing is known of Cree Indians having gone across the line since certain refugees went over after the Half-breed Indian troubles in the Northwest in 1885.

The Indian Commissioner suggests the possibility of refugee French Half-breeds having been confounded with Cree Indians.

The Minister states further with regard to the suggestion made by Mr. Blaine in his letter that the Canadian authorities should co-operate with those of the United States in proper measures for the removal of the Indians in question from the territory of that Government, that they would seem to be no objection, upon the Department of Indian Affairs being advised of the time and place at which any Indian belonging to Canada, who have been guilty of marauding in the United States territory, would be brought to the boundary line, to instructions being sent to the officers of the Northwest Mounted Police to dispatch a detachment of police to the point for the purpose of taking over from the military of the United States the Indians, or such of them, as belong to Canada.

The committee concurring in the above report, recommend that Your Excellency be moved to forward a copy hereof to Her Majesty's Minister at Washington.

All which is respectfully submitted for Your Excellency's approval.

JOHN J. MCGEE.
Clerk of the Privy Council.

EXECUTIVE OFFICE.

No. 168.

CONSULATE GENERAL OF THE UNITED STATES.

OTTAWA, March 10, 1892.

Hon. William F. Wharton,
  Assistant Secretary of State, Washington, D. C.:

Sir: Referring to my dispatch No. 151, of November 27th, 1891, I have now the honor to transmit a copy of the report of the Committee of the Privy Council of Canada on the depredation by a band of Stony Indians of Canada in Montana, in August, 1891, as complained of by the Governor of Montana in his letter dated Helena, October 22, 1891, addressed to the Hon. Secretary of State, a copy of which, with its enclosure, a report from the Surveyor General of Montana, was sent by me to the Hon. Edgar Dewdney, Minister of the Interior, and Superintendent of Indian Affairs for Canada.

I am, Sir,   Your obediant servant,
RICHARD G. LAY,
Consul General.

Enclosures:
  1. Copy of letter of Consul General Lay to Minister of Interior, dated November 3, 1891.
  2. Copy of Letter of Under Secretary of State, dated March 9, 1892.
  3. Copy of a report of a Committee of the Privy Council of Canada, dated February 19, 1892.

CONSULATE GENERAL OF THE UNITED STATES.

OTTAWA, November 3, 1891.

Hon. E. Dewdney, Minister of the Interior, Ottawa:

SIR: I have the honor to transmit herewith a copy of a communication from his Excellency the Governor of Montana, addressed to the Honorable the Secretary of State, dated at Helena, October 22, 1891, accompanied by a letter of the U. S. Surveyor General of Montana (copy herewith) reporting a depredation in August last by a band of Stony Indians from the Northwest Territory of Canada in the State of Montana near McDonald (or Terry) Lake.

The report states that the Indians remained three weeks or more; that at the time of the raid the country was thronged with elk, deer, moose and mountain goats, and that the Indians wholly destroyed this game, which at the time was the "close season."

I am directed by the Department of State to lay this matter before you for such action as the Dominion Government shall deem proper.

I am, Sir, Your Obedient Servant,
RICHARD G. LAY,
Consul General.

DEPARTMENT OF THE SECRETARY OF STATE.

OTTAWA, March 9, 1892.

The Consul General for the United States of America:

SIR—In reply to your letter of the 3rd of November, 1891, covering certain documents, therein described, having reference to certain alleged depredations said to have been committed by a band of Stony Indians, from Canada, and also for the information of your Government in the premises, I have the honor by command of His Excellency the Governor General in Council, to transmit to you, herewith, copy of an approved minute of the Honorable the Privy Council, embodying the views of the Government on the subject mentioned.

I have the honor to be, sir, your obedient servant,

S. A. CATELLIER,
Under Secretary of State.

Certified copy of a report of a committee of the Honorable Privy Council, approved by His Excellency the Governor General in Council, on the 19th February, 1892.

On a report dated 26th January, 1892, from the Superintendent General of Indian Affairs, stating with reference to the letter, dated Ottawa 3rd Nov. 1891, from the Consul General of the United States of America, for the Province of Ontario and to the communication from His Exellency the Governor of Montana enclosed in the Consul General's letter and addressed to the Honorable the Secretary of State, Washington, said communication being dated at Helena, October 22nd, 1891, and to the letter which accompanied the latter document from the United States Surveyor General, of Montana, reporting a depredation in August last by a band of Stony Indians from Canada, in the State of Montana, near McDonald or (Terry Lake.) in which it is stated that the Indians referred to remained three weeks or more, and that at the time of their arrival the country was thronged with elk, deer, moose and mountain goats, and that the Indians wholly destroyed the game during the term of their visit, which was the close season ; that copies of the letter from the Consul General of the United States and of the documents which accompanied it as above described, were forwarded on the 20th of November last to the Indian Commissioner for Manitoba and the Northwest Territories with the request that he would report on the statements contained in these documents and recommend what steps should, in his opinion, be taken to prevent a recurrence of the alleged depredations.

The Minister further states that on the 18th of January last, the Commissioner reported, as a result of careful inquiry made into the statements contained in the papers sent him, that it had been ascertained that a Stony Indian named Dixon had been absent from the Reserve for a year past with a party numbering 25 souls, inclusive of men, women and children, and that since the said Dixon had a wooden leg and the description of the party complained of in the papers forwarded by the Consul General corresponded to that extent with the said Dixon, it seems probable that the party with him was the one referred to as having committed the depredations complained of; that since, however, the said Dixon and his party are in the United States, and are not likely to return this winter, nothing definite can be ascertained as to their connection with the alleged depredations. The Commissioner further reports that a number of Stony Indians admit that they were south of the boundary line during the course of last summer, but they stated that the Indians in whose country they hunted are their friends and raised no objection to their hunting in their country; and these Indians positively deny having killed either moose or red deer; and from what they say it seems altogether probable that the alleged depredations, if committed by Indians from Canada at all, have been greatly exaggerated.

The Minister further observes that the Indian Commissioner states that as respects the best method to adopt to prevent a recurrence of any similar depredations on the part of the Indians from Canada, the most effective measure would in all probability be for the American authorities to cause the Indians from the Canadian side of the line to be turned back when they make their appearance, and the Commissioner is of opinion that if this were done on one or two occasions the Indians would without doubt discontinue their excursions across the boundary line.

The Minister concurs in the recommendation made by the Indian Commissioner for Manitoba and the Northwest Territories, and he further recommends that in replying to the Consul General of the United States, at Ottawa, an expression of regret of the Canadian Government should be given for the depredations said to have been committed by Indians from Canada, and a suggestion made that the steps recommended by the Indian Commissioner for Manitoba and the Northwest Territories, in order to prevent a recurrence of similar depredations, should be adopted by the authorities in the State of Montana.

The Committee recommend that the Secretary of State be authorized to forward a copy of this Minute, if approved, to the Consul General of the United States, at Ottawa, in reply to his letter of the 3rd November, 1891.

JOHN J. MCGEE,
Clerk of the Privy Council.
The Consul General of the United States, Ottawa.

Incursions of Cree Indians.

WAR DEPARTMENT.
WASHINGTON, Sept. 24, 1892.
The Governor of the State of Montana, Helena, Montana:
SIR: I have the honor to acknowledge the receipt of your letter of the

first inst., transmitting copies of correspondence addressed to you by certain citizens of the State of Montana relative to roving bands of Cree Indians from Canada, who are annoying the citizens of the State, and asking that you request the War Department to investigate the matter and cause these Indians to be removed across the border.

In reply you are respectfully advised that a similar complaint was presented to the Department on January 26th, last, by the Honorable the Secretary of State, who enclosed a copy of a letter from the United States District Attorney for Montana, dated January 18th, last, on the subject. The complaint was carefully investigated by the Commanding General of the Department of Dakota, and resulted in showing that such of the Cree Indians as are now within the United States territory are peacefully and usefully employed and that they would be greatly missed in the industries of the country were they removed. For your information the report of that officer in the premises is quoted as follows:

"Enquiry from all the Posts in this Department, on the northern frontier fails to establish that there has been any recent incursion of Cree Indians from Canada. Since 1885 there have been in our territory about two hundred Cree Indians who were political refugees who took part in the Riel rebellion. These have been permitted to remain and have been up to 1887 fed and clothed through the intervention of the Army. When accessions to these Indians from Canada have been discovered they have been expelled, but it has been found difficult to distinguish the political refugees from those who have come to our territory from other causes. In one instance when a party of Crees were forced across the line, numbers of them returned saying they were threatened with arrest in Canada as being implicated in the Riel rebellion.

At the present time the Post Commanders to whom this correspondence has been referred, report that the Cree Indians, men and women, who are in Montana and North Dakota are employed along the line by citizens in wood chopping and laundry and other work. That they are very useful, are well conducted and would be greatly missed in the industries of the country were they now removed. This information comes from citizens."

Very respectfully,
L. A. GRANT,
Acting Secretary of War.

Addresses, Etc.

Accepting a Life-Size Oil Painting Upon Being Inaugurated as Governor, November 8, 1889.

In accepting the gift Governor Toole said, amid applause:

Fellow Citizens and Friends: I thank you most cordially for this splendid presentation. I am not conscious that I was ever as good looking as that portrait. [Applause.] Some of my Republican friends in the State have always insisted on making my personal appearance an issue in every campaign in which I have been a participant. [Applause.] As I look upon your elegant gift and discover how it flatters me, I find some cause for regret that it was not on exhibition sooner. [Applause.] Popular as my friend Commodore Power is, that portrait would have been elected without opposition, [loud applause] and I would have been saved a hard campaign, in which I made some poor speeches, smoked a great many bad cigars and drank a great deal of alkali water. [Laughter and cheers.] It would be in bad taste to criticise your gift, and I suppose I ought to forbear, but I cannot. I have but one criticism to make. If that canvass, instead of containing my portrait, had transferred upon it your pleasing faces, ever to remind me of your generous hearts and devoted friendship I think I would be better pleased. [Applause.] But, of course, I understand that your compliment is not so much to me as to the high office which I have the honor to fill. I accept your splendid gift so gracefully presented with the best wishes for you all, and I only regret that time, place and circumstances do not permit me to pass around "a little something to sustain nature." [Applause.] I hope some time that the occasion may present when my friends can be accorded a more hospitable reception. Until then you must be content with my most sincere thanks and best wishes for your success and prosperity. [Loud and continued applause.]

I am informed that the serenade tendered by the silver cornet band on this occasion, is independent of these ceremonies, and intended as their compliments. I thank them collectively and individually for the sweet music, for which they are justly famous. [Applause.]

I enter to-day upon the discharge of the duties of this high office determined that the peoples' rights shall never be subordinated to private interests or corporate greed; that honest and faithful service shall be exacted from every public official; that our affairs shall be economically administered; that the reins of this virgin Government this day committed to my keeping shall be held without oppression or wrong-doing, and handed over to my successor with precedents worthy to be followed.

With a Constitution in many respects substantially new, with no forms to follow, or beaten paths in which to travel, but with the whole field of action practically undeveloped and unexplored I can see much responsibility and labor attending the first administration of this State's affairs. The prospect, however is made pleasanter by the delightful beginning which brings you here with the assurances and good wishes so eloquently expressed by your spokesman, Mr. Smith. [Prolonged Applause.]

Welcome to Citizens of Idaho Visiting Helena upon the Completion of the Railroad to the Cœur d'Alenes.

The welcome which we give you is more than a friendly one. You are not only our friends and neighbors, but we realize that you are bound to us by a closer tie. Out of the side of Idaho was taken the silver rib that made Montana, and we have always contended that that operation was only a partial success, because it did not extend to and include the Pan Handle. In 1864 we parted company so far as our political anatomy is concerned, and started business on our own account in what was then the Territory and now the State of Montana, but in all the years that have intervened we have not been unmindful of our maternity or ceased to be interested in her prosperity. We are therefore gratified at the hearty response made to our invitation. We are glad to entertain you and hope to avail ourselves of the opportunity which your coming affords to recall the memories of other days and renew the friendship which a quarter of a century of continued separation has neither obliterated nor dimmed. Our citizens who were lately your guests returned full of admiration for your country and instinct with applause for your hospitality. From this intercourse will spring reciprocal, social and business relations that will promote the prosperity of all concerned. The physical conditions of the two sections, the natural arteries of trade that permeate both, and the homogeneity of our respective populations ought to cement our interests forever.

These mighty mountains that surround you, like your own, have been made to tremble at the touch of the miner's blast, the music of the mills within our borders is the same that abounds in your own domain, and from the heated mouths of our smelters come the same steady flow of bullion which you are accustomed to see at home. The great herds of cattle, sheep and horses upon our ranges, the vast fields of grain and the splendid cities that greet you all speak of the rapid and substantial development of our people. These considerations, so apparent to the observant, unite in demanding a closer commercial relation between the Pan Handle and Montana. To this end and the maintenance of an everlasting friendship between us, I have the honor to give you a cordial welcome to Montana. [Applause.]

Upon the Occasion of Laying the Corner Stone of Temple Emanuel at Helena, Montana, October 12, 1890.

Friends and Fellow Citizens: If we endorse the sentiment that man should so live that memory shall be as bright as hope, then he who lends his hand, his heart or his heritage to the erection of another temple, wherein is taught the immortality of the soul, has not lived in vain. With creeds and ceremonies the State has no concern. It does not stop to enquire whether a creed is true or false, falible or infalible, fatuous or well founded, but following the illustrious example of the United States and recognizing the prevailing belief that the oracles of Jehovah are the foundation stones on which all Government is founded and inexorable law is enthroned, our Constitution wisely provided that the free exercise and enjoyment of religious profession and worship without discrimination shall forever hereafter be guaranteed.

These ceremonies, therefore, are in curious contrast with the proscriptive edicts of the Russian Government respecting those professing the Jewish faith, detailed in this morning's dispatches. This is an American spectacle; the image of the national genius; the handiwork of the utilitarian republic based upon the priceless principle that freedom of thought, freedom of speech and the right of individual interpretation are the three great pillars upon which our national liberty is founded and relying upon this, our system of religion and liberty must flourish or fall together. It cannot fail. This country may be shaken from center to circumference by the throes of war and the fires of revolution; its Constitution may be assailed, modified or amended, but as long as our political anatomy is preserved among the nations of the earth, that fundamental principle will remain inviolate and inviolable. Whether we are guided and controlled by some all-seeing eye, some invisible hand, some omnipotent presence, some "still, small voice," or the sound of a great amen; whether our teacher be preacher, priest or rabbi, our lifeboat is afloat upon the same stream of time and headed for the same sublime port, and although the ways of some at times may seem tortuous to others, all are soothed and sus- sustained by the same unfaltering trust in a "hereafter."

"All the subtileties of metaphysics," said Rousseau, "will not make me doubt the immortality of the soul for one single moment; I feel it; I wish it: I hope for it; I will defend it with my latest breath." While it is true that all nations are not in accord as to the methods and forms of expression touching this idea, none are so poor as to be without hope. Abraham, inspired by the hope of the resurrection consoled himself for the sacrifice of his son Isaac; Job, abandoned by all, comforted himself by the conviction that he would rise again from the grave; the Maccabes yielded up submissively their bodies to the executioner, exclaiming, "God will restore them to us." The Greeks, Persians and Egyptians believed in their Elysian fields and in Tartarus, and we learn from Virgil's Æneid of the faith of the Romans; Stanley tells us how in darkest Africa the Hottentott begs that his bow and arrow may be buried with him that he may fight again; the savage fancies that he hears again the voice of the departed one in the rustle of the leaves and in the murmur of the waters; the Chinese place food upon the graves of their dead because they believe the soul needs nourishment. It seems but yesterday and within our own State, that two Cheyenne Indians, robed in their gayest garments and painted in their brightest colors, mounted upon their war horses and chanting their death song, rode fearlessly and furiously down to a certain and terrible death, in the belief that they would rise again, panoplied in all their rude finery, astride the same steeds so carefully and elaborately prepared.

And so it is that church and State are wisely separated and each left to its own destiny.

While this temple here and now about to be inaugurated is to be conducted under the auspices of a distinctive class of our citizens and in accordance with their particular ceremonials its influence, I predict, will be none the less elevating and inspiring. Wherever the light and lesson of civilization has penetrated the virtuous votaries of this vestal venture will be found, and although it is apparent that here under our Constitution is their vine and fig tree, an American statesman, whose fame is far and wide and whose potential influence helped to blaze the way for Montana's statehood has said of our friends that, "wherever they are and whatever they do their harp is still hung upon the willows of exile and they still sing of Jerusalem as the Psalmist sung, 'If I forget thee, Jerusalem, may my hand forget its cunning and my tongue cleave to the roof of my mouth.'"

Conscious of the sacred duty which I have been invited to perform and with a full appreciation of the kindly feeling that suggested me in connection with this important service, I now have the honor of laying the first corner stone of the first Jewish temple in the State of Montana.

Welcome to the Supreme Lodge of Ancient Order of United Workmen in Session at Helena, Montana.

EXECUTIVE OFFICE.

HELENA, Mont., June 15, 1892.

To the Officers and Members of the Supreme Lodge of the Ancient Order of United Workmen:

An engagement in the city of Deer Lodge, made before a change was announced in your programme, will prevent me from personally tendering to your organization the welcome of the State of Montana. I, however, take this method of welcoming you, and with it I promise the genuine hospitality and open-handed cordiality of our people.

We acknowledge the compliment which a session of your Supreme Lodge implies, and regret as much as you can the work of the elements, which has detracted somewhat from your plans and purposes. We hope, however, that the delay which has been occasioned, and the inconvenience which you have suffered, will be smoothed over and counterbalanced by the friendships you will make, and the sights you will see in this mountain country.

If our people ever had any doubt about the consummate judgment and clear foresight of the men comprising the association of the Ancient Order United Workmen, two events have recently transpired to remove the uncertainty, and commend them to the considerate attention and kind regard of our people. The first event to which I allude was the election of our distinguished fellow citizen (Major Kinsley) as Supreme Master of the Order, and the second was the vote by which you determined to hold this Convention in the Bonanza State, and Queen City of the Rocky Mountains.

We are not three years old as a State, and yet the railway, telegraph and postal systems have crowded out primitive methods, progress has spread population over our vast surface, and steam and electricity connect as closely as within one common city. We are in the midst of a gigantic system of

EXECUTIVE OFFICE. 95

irrigation, which will redeem the great body of arid land within our borders, making our crops independent of rainfall, and absolutely certain. We are in a flood of scientific progression in all that pertains to the extraction and reduction of gold, silver and copper ores. We are producing cattle, sheep and horses upon the native grasses of our foothills which are second to none in the country. We are turning our cattle into beef, our mines into money, our fleece into fabrics, and our barley into beer.

Formerly our barley went into bread, but a company of sagacious and wicked New Yorkers detected its superior color and flavor, and behold! What was intended for the "staff of life" is taken east and transformed into as fine a cosmopolitan beverage as ever tangled an intellect or dissipated a fortune. With these and other great enterprises securely anchored in the firm foundation of solid success, we are going to let business take care of itself for a season while we turn to the more agreeable diversion which a series of supreme lodges, conventions, encampments and congresses will afford us.

We trust that you will find time to visit our various cities and witness the marvelous activity and prosperity which everywhere abounds. You will find every county seat in the State but three accessible by railways, and you will be greeted wherever you go, not only by the members of your own fraternity, but you will be accorded a generous reception by the people at large.

The whole State, and every municipality in it, ought to stimulate the growth and prosperity of every well-founded organization which has for its object the improvement of the mental, moral and social condition of the people, but they have a special and common interest in every well-organized and substantial venture, which, upon its termination, leaves some person in the community provided against want and destitution. To this extent the State, and every municipality in it, has a direct interest in the honest and economical management of your, and similar associations, and their consequent growth and prosperity within our limits. It is believed that there are few men in this State who could not, without serious embarrassment, provide against the contingencies I have mentioned. An intelligent observance of the duties of citizenship requires preparation for time as well as eternity. The man who stops to think, surveys the future and maps out the ways before him, seldom fails. Such a man will seldom let a policy lapse, leave a wife in want, or those dependent upon him, in distress.

When every citizen can provide his family against the accidents and misfortunes of life, which a policy for even $2,000 will remedy or repair, public burdens will diminish, poor houses will decrease and taxation will be lessened.

I renew the welcome already extended, and wish for you the largest measure of success in your deliberations, as well as the greatest amount of pleasure which such a visit can afford. I have the honor to be, with great respect, Your obedient servant,

JOS. K. TOOLE,
Governor.

Relation of the State to the Public Schools—1891. Delivered Before the Montana State Teachers' Association.

Everyone is ready to admit in the presence of this company that most all of the wise things that have been said are to be found in the "standard school books," but I will be pardoned, I am sure, if the occasion has suggested to me an older, if not more reliable authority:

"Wisdom hath builded her houses; she hath hewn her seven pillars; she hath killed her beasts; she hath mingled her wine; she hath also furnished her table.

"She hath sent forth her maidens; she crieth upon the highest places of the city, who is so simple let him turn in hither, as for him who wanteth understanding she saith unto him, come eat my bread and drink of the wine which I have mingled."

You have honored us by a generous response to our invitation, and while we are proud of your presence, I will not oppress you with the idle fanfaranade which such an occasion sometimes invites.

The Queen City of Montana, nestling upon the bosom of the majestic mountain which bears her name, famous alike for her

"Maidens fair and gallant men,
Golden sunsets and golden sands,"

has given you a cordial welcome. As a citizen and servant of the State, I gladly join in this public manifestation of our pleasure. Your mission is honorable and your zeal is inspiring. Your presence and your purpose are pregnant with great import for those who would be "wise in their generation."

They emphasize the maxim of the student, "labor *est ipse voluptas*," and admonish us that wisdom does not descend from father to son, like lands, tenements and hereditaments, by inheritance. It is not garnered for gold, leased for love or won at wager. It does not spring forth spontaneously, but comes by accretion, growing, expanding and ripening like vegetation under the genial influence of sunshine, air and moisture. The physical conditions by which these essentials are applied cannot be disregarded.

In order to secure the best harvest the seeds must be sown in the "springtime of life," nurtured in the "sunshine of truth," exposed to the "air of freedom" and irrigated with that true "Pactolian water" that comes by the "sweat of patient labor."

Your profession, like most others, has kept pace with the mighty strides of American progress.

EXECUTIVE OFFICE. 97

In this age of constant competition, inventive genius, stimulating ambition and eminent learning there is no place for mediocre ability. The highest order of talent is everywhere in demand. Veneering no longer passes for solid wood. Stimulated learning will not supply the place of wisdom. The indolent, the indifferent and the sluggard drop out of the procession, or fall defenseless beneath it. You stand here as sponsors for the State, her tireless and vigilant sentinels, the exponents of her wisdom in committing us irrevocably to the public school system.

By the concensus of opinion, based upon close observation and long experience, our system of public schools, although it has not attained perfection is the most complete and capable of exerting the greatest good to the greatest number of any similar institution under the Government. It is peculiarly an American system. It is the safe repose of the citizen, the indispensible condition of our Constitution, and the beacon light of our Nation whose power and perpetuity are made to rest upon the consent of the governed. The whole system, freighted with the gravest interests and watched with the most jealous solicitude, is committed largely to your keeping.

If under your fostering care and influence it shall grow and expand to the proportions of our just expectations, there will be a corresponding compensation in the fact that your name and fame will be commensurated with its achievements.

Aside from this you will have justified the confidence reposed in you by the public. I have no fear for the future with these interests in your hands.

I have been a passive, but interested observer of your proceedings from year to year, and have noted the enthusiasm and energy which have attended your deliberations. What I have seen preverifies the prediction that you are destined to prove a tower of strength in moulding the thought, and shaping the policy of the State in years to come. Cartain is it that your influence will be wide-spread and far-reaching in that direction. We are accustomed to boast of the richness of our mines of gold, silver, lead, copper and iron. We talk glibly of our rank ranges, fat cattle, fast horses, fine flocks, fertile fields, fabulous forests, majestic mountains, sunny skies, wonderful waters and still more wonderful winds, sometimes of silky softness, spice-laden from the tropics, and known to us as the blessed "Chinook," but these alone do not constitute a State. National wealth is not the only standard of greatness, nor the "*sumum bonum*" of the citizen. Daniel was once called upon by a mighty citizen to repeat and interpret a forgotten dream. The prophet declared that the vision which the king had seen in the night, and which he had vainly attempted to recall, bodied forth a colossal figure, the head of which was of gold, the arms and waist of silver, the rest of the body of brass, the legs of iron and clay. We are told that a stone from a mountain dashed down against it and ground it to pieces, and the wind blew against it and it was no more.

This formidable figure mounted upon a pedestal of copper fringed with lead, does not inaptly represent the principal resources that decorate our State, but these will not satisfy our State's demands. Something else must be added or we shall not be unlike a certain Roman maiden, who fell a victim to the weight of her own ornaments. The true test of human greatness is found, not in riches alone, but in the intellectuality, the morality and the patriotism of the people, the boys and girls, the men and women of the State.

It is yours to inculcate and maintain these public virtues in a great measure in your capacity as teachers. To this end the State will not only lend you its sympathy and encouragement, but will bring to your support its munificent fund of land and money. With all these favorable conditions I shall be surprised if there does not go forth from this superb mountain land a citizenship peerless and priceless, whose voice will be heard and whose influence will be felt whenever the State needs a champion or the Nation a defender.

I trust the time will not be long delayed when our State University, Agricultural College and School of Mines shall be a part of the permanent institutions of the State. I would not circumscribe the possibilities of the most thorough and complete education attainable, but I believe in an American education for an American citizen. If our institutions of learning do not reach the acme of perfection we should not relax our efforts until they have attained it. We have demonstrated that the children of Montana in point of intellect and physical development are second to none in the world. Their opportunities should be co-extensive with their capabilities. The boys and girls of this State, who are to be the beneficiaries of your wisdom may not be as quick at "repertoire" as some of their more fortunate brothers and sisters, who, spurning American culture, go across the waters to gather knowledge, and returning affect rejoicing that their feet are once more upon America's "terra cotta," convulse their friends with rapturous descriptions of the "Venus de Medicine," the "Appollo Belladona," the "bust" of somebody's hand and display with pride their bric-a-brac made of the finest "terra firma" or the latest "larvae" from Vesuvius, or a picture of themselves by one of the "old master masons," but I do not doubt that they will be wiser in the ways of the world and less ridiculous in the face of their friends.

I have in mind a man with a rich father who determined that his son should have all the advantages which wealth could give, and so he hied him away to Heidelberg, and all other Bergs across the water. He came back to his native town an accomplished spendthrift and an alleged lawyer. His law office was furnished with a beautiful library in Greek, German and French, but not an English or American edition was to be found in the list.

His clientage did not swell in numbers as he expected and his talents soon developed in another direction. The rod and gun, the race course and the prize ring charmed him most. His library of gilded authors soon fell into *inocusus desuetude* and his office was abandoned, and this was all because his learning was superficial. If he had set his pride aside and yielded to truth

he could have exclaimed with the Earl of Warwick, when appealed to for legal advice by Sumerset and Plantaganet,
"Between two hawks, which flies the higher pitch?
Between two dogs, which hath the deeper mouth?
Between two blades, which bears the better temper?
Between two horses, which doth bear him best?
Between two girls, which hath the merriest eye?
I have perhaps, some shallow spirit of judgment.
But in these nice sharp quillets of the law,
Good faith, I am no wiser than a daw."
The list of such could be extended indefinitely, but I forbear.

I wish you continued success and prosperity in the great field of endeavor before you, and assure you of the State's cordial co-operation in your work and warm welcome upon this occasion.

Commencement Exercises of the Montana College, Deer Lodge, Montana, June 16th, 1892.

While acknowledging the high compliment which your invitation to address you implies, it was by no means probable a day or two ago that I could hope to do so. The demands upon my time growing out of official duties had been so great as to preclude the possibility of more than a bare suggestion touching these ceremonies, and after observations respecting college education in connection with the duties of citizenship. These exercises mark another mile-stone in the great field of progress and civilization that sorrounds us. Every commencement day is a new inspiration, leading many of us back through visions of beauty, and pointing the way to others in the realm of realities yet unseen. It was a wise forethought that conceived the idea of establishing the college of Montana in this beautiful city and mountain encircled valley. It did not start, as I remember, under the most favorable circumstances, but the rapid progress which it has made shows how firmly it has established itself in the confidence and regard of the people.

The latest fruits of her endeavor are seen here to-day; as three of her children take leave of their Alma Mater strong in the confidence of self support ; fortified and sustained by the conscious pride that animates the first flush of manhood. We are here by kind invitation to welcome with our presence and plaudits those who have succeeded so well to the great domain of energy, labor and usefullness.

Such an occasion is full of interest. In the Egypt of the Ptolomies three thousand years ago, it was their custom to appoint magistrates to judge the memory of the deceased citizen, and to award, to prince and peasant alike, condemnation to the vicious, and to the virtuous, the honors of a public eulogy. Instead of judges sitting in solemn quest over the ashes of the dead, we assemble, I believe in far better taste, to offer our admirations and congratulations at the supreme hour when life begins in earnest. You, gentlemen, who have so honorably acquitted yourselves will continue to be objects of interest to our people. Let us hope that you will hold up without reproach in the battle of life the noble standard which this institution teaches and applauds.

This event emphasised the advantage which the man of education possesses over the large majority who either cannot, or refuse to, accept the benefits which the college offers. Armed and equipped with the knowledge which such an institution supplies, the graduate is prepared for an intelligent participation in the functions of Government.

A recent paper published by Mr. Arthur Comey, in an educational journal shows to what extent college education is appreciated.

He shows that the number of male students attending 282 colleges in various parts of the United States had nearly doubled in the decade between 1880 and 1890, though the increase in population during the same period had been only 25 per cent. He showed also in a series of clear and most carefully compiled tables that between 1850 and 1890 the number of male students in these colleges had increased from 8,837 to 31,359; that while the increase in population during that period had been 165 per cent., the increase in the number of students had been 254 per cent.; and that the number of students per 100,000 of population had risen from 38.1 in 1850 to 50.3 in 1890.

In making up his tables, Mr. Comey ommitted all students in the preparatory courses of many Southern and Western colleges, and all women in the educational institutions. He ommitted also a few colleges on account of low standard, and all the scientific schools, though he included scientific students in colleges. Had he included the scientific schools which have been organized almost wholly since 1860, the percentage of increase would have been far greater than appears from his tables. His conclusions are that the "colleges of the country are growing rapidly," that "there is at the same time a decided tendency to raise the standard both for admission and for the courses of study," and that these facts justify " even uptimistic views of the future of higher education."

That time when—

"All crimes shall cease, and ancient fraud shall fail,
Returning justice lift aloft her scale;
Peace o'er the world her olive wand extend,
And white-robed innocence from heaven descend."

It will not do to sit down and wait for this sweet time to come, nor yet forget that the purity and growth of our society and institutions depend largely upon keeping up the standard of intelligence, efficiency and morality of the masses of the people.

To accomplish this in any appreciable degree depends not only upon the proper intellectual training of our population, but the statesmen of our country must furnish us immediate relief against the indiscriminate influx of the vicious and pauper contributions of other countries. We should extend a cordial welcome to all who come in search of homes, and whose education and instincts promise an attachment to our form of Government, and who are properly qualified to earn an honest living, but for those who have no respect for our laws; no regard for instructions; no toleration for our religions, we have no place in this great republic.

While we boast of a free country, let it never be said that freedom implies indolence, disregard of the rights of others, or a land where the vices of men are unrestrained. Ours is a country of free thought, free speech and free interpretation, but it is a country where success rests upon the bed-rock of honest toil and obedience to law. It may be that in the ages yet to be unfolded, our increasing knowledge of the secrets of nature may enable us to escape much of the drudgery that is now the daily fate of the vast majority of mankind, and place the whole race upon a higher plane of intelligence, but for the present we must avail ourselves of the best means at our command. We cannot therefore hope that more than a small minority can ever receive the benefits of a college education. It is this minority, however, that is to leaven the mass. While it is true that all free government is democratic in theory, it is necessarily aristocratic in fact. The few must administer it. Our constitutional guarantee of freedom, therefore, amounts to nothing more than that the few who administer it are not permanently entrenched behind the ramparts of privilege, but are subject to change, that the men of to-day are not the men of yesterday, and that it is always in the power of the majority to discard the old and appoint new administrators of the powers of government. And so it is that if republics would perpetuate themselves, they must promote the virtues and foster the education of their citizens. Let us do our part fairly in this great work. Let us frown down bribery and corruption, and put the seal of condemnation upon every attempt to interpolate the principles of the pirates into American politics.

We are accustomed to hear appeals to the passions and prejudices of men instead of their judgments, to the lurid insanity of sectional hatred or the more dangerous prejudice of foreign nationality. We have seen the beautiful theory of universal suffrage used to degrade the powers of the Government into the hands of the worst element of society, and we have seen the honor of the bench and the integrity of the jury abandoned at the behest of the depraved and merciless Maffia until there was evolved that worst of tyranies, the tyrany of the mob as the justification for the taking of human life.

There is a prevalent political philosophy that all these evils will right themselves in the course of time. Let us hope that the wonderful elasticity of our composite race justifies the prediction, but there are others who are bold enough to believe and declare that political corruption must eventuate in national degredation, civil decay and Cæserism. For the want of education we fail to see that we are repeating humanity's sad story, and that the causes that overthrew the republics of Israel and of Athens, and of Rome, of Italy and of the Netherlands, are precisely the same causes that are to-day threatening the foundations of our free institutions. It is agreed that we need the higher education here; we need the education both of the intellect and the heart to guard against these evils before it is too late, for the former without the latter may make us accomplished criminals, and the latter without the former only amiable idiots.

In education all thoughtful men now see the only remedy for the evils of our time, and the only solution for the many problems that now perplex us. But even those who laud it most, says a distinguished jurist of our times, do not tell us how education is to solve these problems, how education is to bridge the widening chasm between capital and labor, or to reconcile the growing conflict between co-operative combination and individual freedom. We have seen the conflict between capital and labor widening and expanding until it is doubtful whether the strain can much longer exist. Who will answer for the result when that time shall come calling organized labor into simultaneous action? There must be something wrong in a system that brings its annual strikes and requires armed men in secret service to stand guard over persons and property. No one denies that property is entitled to protection; that principle is fundamental. Our national history is pregnant with the evidences of our convictions in this regard and records many a heroic struggle to protect the owner in the enjoyment of his property rights. The rights of labor are not plain and are not conceeded. The great writ of right of 1679 defined and secured the liberty of the citizen and being secure now in his civil rights he demands a hearing as to the disposition of his labor. No less a person than Gladstone has declared that the Constitution of the United States is the grandest instrument which was ever struck off by the hand and brain of man, and yet the framers of this instrument could not foresee every condition that might be evolved by a progressive and acquisitive people. When the laws of entail were enacted they did not dream of wealth in shares. Wealth in acres was the standard. Corporations were unknown. Capital and labor must be independent. Legislation can never make them equal. A paternal Government is a failure.

But intelligence is not itself a remedy, nor does it immediately supply the remedy. Neither is it the intelligent who have been the most virtuous, and ignorance has not always been the worst enemy of our race. The World's most dangerous men are the Cæsars, the Robspierres and the Bonapartes, the men of intelligence and education without virtue and honor; the men, who, by that combination of gift and deficiency, are enabled most lavishly to do on earth the work of hell and bring untold misery upon their fellowmen. The bloodiest ruffianism of the French revolution, we are told emanated from the hands of men of education and women of supposed refinement.

The best educated Sovereign that has ever occupied the throne of England from the Norman conquest to the present time, was the brutal tyrant, Henry the VIII. Timur was one of the most learned of Asiatic rulers, and a lecture which I heard a year ago by Dr. Milburn, satisfied me that our own country has produced no more accomplished a man than Aaron Burr. And

EXECUTIVE OFFICE.   103

yet education, higher education, must solve the complications of Government, but, as before suggested, the sentimental side of our natures must keep pace with the intellectual.

No less a judge of men than Napoleon Bonaparte said that imagination governed the world, meaning thereby the sentimental faculties in man, and he never said a truer thing. It was upon this theory that most of his good deeds and many of his bad ones are based; upon this theory he founded the Legion of Honor; upon this theory he sought to dazzle the world rather by the splendor than the solidity of his enterprises. It is the sentimental and intellectual that governs the great heart of humanity.

The federal Government has endowed us with a generous donation of public lands, for school purposes. These lands are being sold and leased as rapidly as the demand affords. The principal under the Constitution remains inviolable, the interest only being used. With the increase in the value of these lands and the taxable property of the State, I predict that no State in the Union will be in a condition to prepare her children to enter college so cheaply and so well as the State of Montana.

We have many men in this State who have gathered from her treasures wealth beyond the possibilities of expenditure in the ordinary course of life. What a grand field the endowment of educational institutions offers to such! The late Col. Chas. A. Broadwater, whose death is lamented by a whole State, had in mind such a noble purpose. And having mentioned this fact to his old friends in this city, the scene of his earliest exploits, I am asked in conclusion to pay a tribute to his memory. A brief reference may stimulate others to emulate his example.

Let it be written that Charles A. Broadwater was a self-made man, that he was courageous and chivalric, and as befits the brave he was instinct with kindness, considerate of the poor and never oppressed the weak. He was hospitable to strangers and princely to his friends. He did not look at the exterior, but the interior qualifications of the man. He believed that if the touch-stone was applied to every life some noble sentiment would respond. And so it was that among those who loved him were found many men in whom others could see no good.

He was of gentle blood, but there was enough iron in it to resent a wrong, and an open foe did well to guard with caution and watch with apprehension; but when the sun went down upon a battle finished, every record was expunged, and every memory was obliterated in the fragrant fumes of the pipe of peace. He did not meddle with small affairs, but grappled with great enterprises. He was at all times amiable and plausible. His fame as a pioneer builder and potent factor in business and politics was widespread. I cannot undertake to recount his successes or review a career so remarkable and so prolific of great results to this State, but if I had the power of condensation and statement I might do so, for I have seen him grow from the adventurous and restive period of life into the strength and symmetry of rugged manhood, from the wagon boss to the presidency of a great railroad, from the hard-pressed borrower to the generous lender, from the private to the public benefactor, from obscurity to fame. All along this steady pathway of progression there was no fulsome fanfaronade, no patronizing air, no supercilious look, no conscious pride to obstruct his march or dim the glory of his achievements.

His life and works show the great possibilities that wait on well directed thoughts and stimulated energies. He never made up his mind to do a thing until he had considered it well and counted all the chances, and, having determined, no man ever knew him to abandon a project or desert a cause. He deserves the commendation of one gifted with more than poetic inspiration, who has said:

"All my life long
I have beheld with most respect the man
Who knew himself and knew the ways before him,
And from amongst them choose considerately,
With a clear foresight, not a blindfold courage,
And, having chosen, with a steadfast mind
Pursued his purpose."

He had many projects in mind for the betterment and upbuilding of the city that he was always proud to call his home, and so fortified were we in the confidence which his endorsement and aid inspired that we were prone to consider them half accomplished. No man can approximate the good he would have done had he lived for twenty years more. What an array of witnesses we would call to testify to his devoted friendship, his genuine kindness, his broad charity, his reassuring advices, his wide philanthropy!

I do not say that he was without imperfections. I would not set him up on cold unyielding pedstal of severest criticism and pursue his life to the last and final analysis without the expectation of finding some clouded canopy, some dreary desert, some waste place. I would not measure the life and character of any man warm-hearted, impulsive, aspiring, whose dawn of manhood opened on a far frontier, and whose habits were shaped and formed in the midst of great activities, by the superfine standard of a dreamer, or the Utopian idea of a moralist. I would prefer to judge him by the elastic line of a common-sense man who can recognize the obligations of morality without a tinge of asceticism, and who can observe all the just proprieties without engaging in Pecksniffian pretense.

His daily life, in the sweet abandon of boon companionship, afforded the best opportunity to know that his heart was warmed by the rays of the ancient faith, and that the best criterion by which to judge him is not by his professions, but by his works.

"'Tis not the wide phylactery,
The subborn fast, nor stated prayers
That makes us saints: We judge the tree
By what it bears."

It is reserved for others to spread upon memorial pages the complete history of the life and character of this brave pioneer, worthy citizen and true friend. Many there are whom he has loaded with the proof of his esteem who will gladly do it. I have only spoken of him in the abstract; I cannot pursue the subject further and restrain the flow of natural emotions. It is due to those who survive him to say that the symmetry of our friend's well rounded career was not wanting in the harmonious complement of a prosperous wedlock. No one can tell how much of his success was due to this happy union. A son and daughter survive to comfort their widowed mother.

We have laid him to rest in the place consecrated to the dead. It is unlike the enchanted spot from which we bore him, but the great white sentinels that surround him in the City of the Dead are the silent monitors that sooner or later we must all meet upon a common level. We shall not soon forget our friend.

When, in after years, the soil of the great Milk River Valley, which he explored and brought to the attention of the directors of the Great Northern railway company, shall have responded to the plow of the sturdy husbandman, and waving fields of grain shall delight the eyes; when St. Paul, Great Falls, Helena, Butte, and Kalispel shall have realized the full fruitition of the hopes that were inspired by the connecting bands of steel which his wisdom conceived and his foresight and energy made possible; when Fort Harrison, which he did so much to establish, shall have been constructed in accordance with our just expectations, and from its spires, pointing away into the depth of ether, shall float the starry emblem of the great republic; and, finally, when the springtime comes around and I attend each opening of the famous natatorium that bears his name, a poem in its construction and a palace in its appointments, his chosen place to live and die, and I behold the ash, the maple and the elm that he transplanted, put on their garniture of green, and the shrubs and vines that a Shenstone might admire, swaying in the circumambient air, and the many flowers that he loved unfolding their tinted beauties to the radiant sun, and the great green sward with its rustic seats and winding ways shining like an oasis in a doleful desert, and crystal fountains shooting limpid sprays amid the fragrance that abounds, and the mirrored lake reflecting the peaceful mountain in the west, and sportive children bathing in the soft glow of prismatic colors that dance across the imprisoned waters, and when I view contented groups of men and women in shady places wander and listen to the strains of low, sweet music that delighted him so much, and hear the unanimous acclaim, "he builded better than he knew," may I remove my hat and in a reverential calm remember him who out of chaos wrought all of this and more for us; remember him whose eye always beamed at the sight of beauty and moistened at the sound of a sigh.

Welcome to the Members of the National Mining Congress in Session at Helena, Montana, July 12, 1892.

We realize that many of you, with more or less personal sacrifice, have traveled a long distance in response to our invitations to hold the second session of the National Mining Congress in this State. Those who have honored us with their presence are given a cordial welcome. We feel that there is a peculiar fitness in such a body holding its session in the very heart of the greatest mineral producing section of the world. The great west which has contributed so much to the wealth of the nation and received so little in return, will have an opportunity to here formulate her claims and present them before the people of the country. They will rest upon no weak or measly plea of the mendicant, but upon the substantial demand for justice. This will be the legitimate domain for discussion of everything that pertains to mining. In it will necessarily be involved the great question which agitates not only the National Congress, but the whole country, the free and unlimited coinage of silver. With distinguished representatives here from every section of the country, it is not improbable that many different views will be expressed and plausibly maintained.

I desire to express the hope that remedies for confessed financial evils will be suggested, and that the present inequality between the metalic moneys of the Constitution will be speedily corrected; that the insufficient volume of money per capita shall be increased to meet the demands of a great and growing population. It has been stated, no doubt with levity, that the scarcity of the volume of money is not in fact a real difficulty, but that the trouble lies in the scarcity of the volume of collateral. We will know more of this as the business of this Congress progresses.

Distinguished and learned gentlemen here will tell us whether it is true or not, that it is practicable or possible for Europe to give up its silver product, and if it is, whether the silver which we would receive would increase the volume of money, per capita, to more than is necessary to meet the demand of our population? Directly connected with this is the problem how to bridge the widening chasm between capital and labor? How to bridge the growing conflict between co-operative combination and individual freedom? There is a prevalent political philosophy that all of these evils will right themselves in due course of time. Let us hope then, that the wonderful elasticity of our composite race will justify the prediction, but I am credulous enough to believe that as long as less than three per cent of the entire population possess more than two-thirds of the wealth of the world, this struggle will go on growing in intensity and gathering momentum until no power can resist the fury of the contention. There is no method by which hoarded wealth, acquired under the forms of law, can be diffused throughout the channels of trade and commerce, except by the consent of those who own it; but there is a palpable and easy remedy in my humble opinion by enlarging the volume of currency so that the average man will have an incentive to labor for more than a mere existence.

I maintain that with the present restricted volume of currency, and lodged where it is, in the hands of a few, relief is impracticable, if not impossible, by any other method. However this may be, these and kindred questions are submitted for your consideration, discussion and determination. Wishing you a harmonious session and having full confidence in your wisdom, I predict that your action, whatever it may be, will sooner or later be vindicated by the whole people. I renew the welcome already extended to this hospitable State.

Welcome to the Sons of Veterans Holding a National Encampment at Helena, Montana. 1892.

I have been invited to extend to you the welcome of Montana. I do it with pleasure and assure you it is universal, cordial and continuous. We welcome you because we delight to entertain the stranger, and tell him of the wealth and wonders of this new State.

It is said that no man ever left it willingly, or was happy until he returned. Whether it be the health and vigor of our climate, our lofty mountains, rich valleys, stately pines, fresh air, pure water, mineral wealth, sparkling sapphires, gallant men or beautiful women, or all of these combined that infatuates, I do not undertake to say, but certain it is that some of these will claim you as their own if your power of resistance is not greater than the average stranger. But, aside from this, we welcome you for what you are and what you represent.

Your patrimony may take wings and depart forever, professional and business enterprises may fail you, health and strength may degenerate and leave you debendent, and finally when the sun goes down on the battle finished you may be gathered to the tomb, but there is comfort and glory in the reflection that even the grave is not wide enough or deep enough to hide the honor that belongs to a soldier's son who emulates the virtues of his father.

Commencing with the order of the Cincinnati, which sprang from the fires of the revolution a long array of societies might be paraded to illustrate the devotion of the American people to those heroes who contributed to the establishment and perpetuation of civil liberty in this country. As I understand its origin and object, none had a worthier inception or fulfills a more patriotic purpose than the "Sons of Veterans." Through your organization the purposes of laudable ambitions are transmitted from generation to generation, public and private virtues are kept untarnished and love of country is blended with the love of those who gave force and character to a great cause. In that awful emergency their value was supreme, their endurance was superhuman, their suffering was intense, their confidence was abiding, their victory was complete, but their reward remained in what prophetic vision had portrayed, a peaceful, prosperous and united country. Whatever was worthy of accomplishment in that great struggle is worthy of commemoration, not in the narrow sense of kindling anew the dead flame of sectional animosity, but in the larger sense that we may be thankful far more than exultant over the achievements of the men to whom you are so closely related by the ties of blood and affection.

Many a delusion, many a false prophecy and many a harsh declaration has been stilled by the conflict of arms, and they are buried forever among the errors of the past, to be remembered only that they may be avoided hereafter.

You will find in this mountain land many kindred spirits and loyal friends. In this teeming and fruitful west we count our patriots as we count our people. If from any cause the honor or reputation of the nation should again be assailed or imperiled and the dread alarm of war should be sounded, I predict that the contingent from Montana headed by the "Sons of Veterans," inspired by the memories of the past, would be swift to follow if not to lead in just defense.

Every state in the union and nearly every nation of the earth has contributed to the cosmopolitan population that greets you. They——

"Crossed the prairies, as of old their fathers crossed the sea,
To make the West, as they the East, the homestead of the free."

Every one of these is instinct with applause for the deeds which have made your fathers conspicuous among men, and will elaborate and emphasize as occasion offers the brief welcome which it has been my pleasure to extend.

www.ingramcontent.com/pod-product-compliance
Lightning Source LLC
Chambersburg PA
CBHW020145170426
43199CB00010B/889